About the Author

Ash Narain Roy is Assistant Editor at *The Hindustan Times*, New Delhi. Dr Roy, who holds a doctorate from the Jawaharlal Nehru University, specialises in Indian politics, foreign affairs, and in particular Latin American issues. A fluent Spanish and Portuguese speaker, in 1980-84, he spent four years at the prestigious Centro de Estudios Internacionales, El Colegio de Mexico, as a visiting scholar. He has also been associated with the journal, *Third World*, which is published from Rio de Janeiro and Mexico City. Over the years, he has been given several awards and fellowships, including as first recipient of the Appan Menon Memorial Award.

The Third World in the Age of Globalisation:
Requiem or New Agenda?

Ash Narain Roy

Madhyam Books
Delhi

Zed Books
London & New York

The Third World in the Age of Globalisation: Requiem or New Agenda? was published in South Asia by Madhyam Books, 142 Maitri Apartments, Plot No. 28, Patparganj, Delhi - 110 092, in 1999.

ISBN 81 86816 11 9 (pb)

Published outside South Asia by Zed Books Ltd., 7 Cynthia Street, London, N1 9JF and Room 400, 175 Fifth Avenue, New York, NY 10010, USA in 1999.

Distributed in the United States exclusively by St Martin's Press, Inc., 175 Fifth Avenue, New York, NY 10010, USA.

ISBN 1 85649 795 X (hb)
     1 85649 796 8 (pb)

A catalogue record for this book is avaliable from the British Library.

US CIP has been applied for from the Library of Congress.

Printed and bound in India by Gopsons Papers Ltd., Noida.
Cover design by Brij Raj Goel.

Contents

Preface

At the end of the millennium, the world seems to be facing paradigm shifts. Anxiety and disorientation are one result, but one also feels a sense of opportunity and hope. Can we detect an emerging global order in the trends of world economics and politics today? Can we successfully identify the underlying forces, the fundamental sources of change, which will shape events in the next century? After a century of global wars and nearly 50 years of Cold War, the world has entered an era when wars among the major powers seem a near-impossibility despite NATO's barbaric air attacks against Yugoslavia; but wars among and within the smaller nation-states threaten to become even more intense than before.

The world is on the cusp of new ideological and economic paradigms. Every country in the world is being asked to fit the same model. If liberal democracy is the model which has found a near universal acceptability, the market-oriented economic reform is the new creed. Ironically, market economy is already in deep trouble in many places even if its triumph is proclaimed. If the economy fails, can democracy be a success?

Until recently, the primary engine of conflict in international politics was the East-West divide. Today, it is the North-South split. The development gap between the rich and poor nations has created a new duality in the world. The computer and digital highway represent the basis for a new industrial revolution to match those built on steam, the railways and the internal combustion engine. This is bound to cause dislocation all around just as previous periods of dramatic industrial change did.

Where does the Third World find itself in the emerging global order? Has the Third World ideology run out of steam? Are Non-Alignment and other Third Worldist ideologies the concepts whose time has passed? Is it the time to write an obituary of the Third World? What is the agenda before the Third World in the 21st century? This book makes an attempt to answer some of these questions.

The focus of the book is primarily Latin America which enjoys a unique place in the Third World. Latin America's genius, they say, is its own survival. First the Europeans and later the United States sought to trample through it, stealing the Indians' language, their gods and their ravishing innocence. But as Latin American history bears out, it has refused to play the victim. Latin America's genius is in not giving up its gods but in taking the enemy's gods as its own. Latin America is a place of rape which became marriage and of European intrigue which became romance.

Every land has its tragedy. Europe's has been class and nation, America's race and Latin America's politics – the politics of anti-politics. But then, there is no growing, no learning without pain and failure. Latin America's national cultures coincide with the physical limits of each one of its nations even as its larger cultural boundaries embrace the Iberian peninsula and through it Europe. Latin American culture which is so varied—European, Indian and black—does not propose religious fundamentalism or ethnic intolerance. If nuclear weapons have never found a fertile terrain in Latin America, it speaks of the peaceful vocation of the region. Few regions in the world have a greater experience in diplomatic negotiation than Latin America as a result of its difficult dealings with its powerful northern neighbour. This has created a cultural tradition that stresses peaceful solution of controversies, diplomacy and adherence to international laws and treaties.

It is therefore surprising and somewhat intriguing that a region with such credentials should have remained on the margins of Third World politics. Latin American States have often been seen to be breaking ranks with the Third World when their self-interests and Third World solidarity come in conflict.

Latin America's democratic advance since the 1980s has been significant and impressive. In recent years incumbent administrations have yielded office to elected opponents in countries as diverse as Argentina, Bolivia, Ecuador, Uruguay and the Dominican Republic – in some cases for the first time in history. In economics as in politics, events in Latin America have often caught observers by surprise. The region has gone from being the fuse of the debt bomb that threatened the international financial system to being a powerful magnet for global capital. Almost overnight one of the most protectionist regions in the world has become one most open to trade.

Latin America's transformation is nothing short of an ideological revolution. And yet, its democratic roots are still shallow. In some cases new democracies have initiated only the rudiments of democratic institutions. Elected executives lack effective control over the military. Legislatures are weak and poorly financed. Legal systems lack the training, resources and authority to protect human rights and due process of law. Also missing is the cultural and civic infrastructure of democracy and independent, pluralist mass media. More importantly, Latin American societies remain heavily bifurcated and characterised by a European, wealthy elite in policy making positions on the one hand and a non-European, poor, marginalised population on the other.

A study such as this owes a great deal to sharing the thoughts of others in print, discussions in seminars and conversations with a host of academics, journalists, diplomats and others over a period of time. I was greatly inspired to undertake a serious research project on the Third World, particularly Latin America's role in it, while doing my doctoral work at the Centro de Estudios Internacionales, El Colegio de Mexico, Mexico City during the early 1980s. Since that time I built up a long list of related resource materials on the subject and always cherished writing a book. Happily, when I informed my editor, Mr V N Narayanan, about my desire to apply for the Appan Menon Memorial Trust Award, it was he who suggested the subject. I would like to gratefully acknowledge the encouragement Mr Narayanan gave me to pursue this project.

I felt extremely honoured and privileged to receive the first Appan Menon Memorial Trust Award for the year 1997-98. This study was made possible only by this grant. Throughout the process of writing this book, I incurred many intellectual as well as other debts too numerous to mention here. I am grateful to all those who shared with me their concerns about Latin America and the Third World. I am thankful to Latin American diplomatic missions in New Delhi for providing necessary support in pursuing this work. I owe a special debt of gratitude to Mr Edmundo Font, Ambassador of Mexico to India and Mr Gerardo M. Biritos, Ambassador of Argentina to India for having been generous with their time and discussing a wide-range of issues pertaining to Latin America's role vis-à-vis the Third World. I am extremely thankful to Mexican Foreign Ministry for a 5-week invitation to lecture at El Colegio de Mexico and other universities in March 1999. I am grateful to Professor Issam El-Zaim of El Colegio de Mexico for his insightful comments on the future of the Third World.

I am specially grateful to Ms Purba Dutt whose comments on the first draft were stimulating and unfailingly sharp which enriched my understanding of the subject. Particular thanks are due to my wife Dina who constantly stood by me to make up for my inadequacy in the art of word processing. My 8-year-old daughter Martina kept reminding me of my progress all through the completion of this book. I am equally indebted to Mr Shelbi Joseph for his assistance in the preparation of this book in camera ready form. Particular thanks are due to Mr Kavaljit Singh of Madhyam Books and Robert Molteno of Zed Books for their keen interest in the book.

Finally, the debt I owe to my parents defies any description in words and for the fear of rendering it formal, I prefer to leave it at its source — the very depths of my inner self.

New Delhi   Ash Narain Roy

1

Introduction

Revolutionaries are usually the last people to grasp that they are past
their sell - by date. Third Worldism, once a reigning ideology in much of
the developing world is, today, in disarray, and Third World politics or
'Third World-ness' is adrift. The Non-Aligned Movement (NAM) was
once a beacon for Third World countries in their fight for freedom, world
peace, justice and human welfare. Presently, with the United States the
only superpower left, and Russia still smarting from its dramatic loss of
world power status, NAM and the protagonists of Third Worldism are
scrambling to show they are not sitting pointlessly out on a limb.

The Third World politics is facing not just a mid-life but possibly a
terminal crisis. It is no longer possible to look at world developments
from the point of view of superpower rivalries today, for this paradigm
has lost its relevance in the post-Cold War era. Whichever way one
looks at the contemporary world, the realisation is gradually dawning on

Third World leaders that the ideology of Third Worldism has run out of steam. There is of couse a myopic refusal on the part of some leaders to acknowledge that Third Worldism has lost its relevance, at least in the way it was played during the Cold War era.

The dilemma facing the Third World in the post-Cold War, post-nationalist world is similar to what committed revolutionaries often face "without a revolution". Jacques Derrida calls it an "aporia". With no available options desirable, Derrida maintains, "one confronts an aporia, an undecidable and ungrounded political space, where no path is clear and green, where no certain knowledge opens up the way in advance, where no decision is already made". The Third World is confronted with a situation where the old world order is not desirable, but the new world order has not yet been born.

Most ideologies, movements and theoretical formulations of the 20th century have been discredited by historical events. It happened with Marxism-Leninism and it happened with neo-liberalism. In fact, if Communism is the god that failed the Left, neo-liberalism as symbolised by Margaret Thatcher and Ronald Reagan is the god that failed conservatism. Failure of socialism in Eastern Europe and elsewhere in the world led people like Francis Fukuyama to proclaim the "end of history". But if socialism is dead as is commonly believed, the neo-liberal horse too has become anaemic. Reasons for the failure of the two were somewhat similar. Both Marxism and neo-liberal analyses of the problem were largely at odds with their prescriptions for change.

If socialism left virtually everything to the state and the state sector, the New Right assumed individuals to be acting as rational agents. Socialists' over-confidence in the state and neo-liberals' total lack of it proved rather flawed. While states of all ideological and economic colours – liberal, conservative, authoritarian, social democratic, fascist, capitalist or otherwise – went on accumulating more and more powers, neo-liberals did not allow the state even selective intervention in the generation of growth. Neo-liberalism, indeed, became a theology. The Non-Aligned Movement too has fallen into disrepute in the post-Cold War world, because of a paradigm shift. NAM, of course, still organises grand international junkets. The host country still tries to squeeze every drop of prestige from NAM proceedings. But the movement has been virtually reduced to a lobby group for poorer nations.

I. Explanatory Paradigm

The term 'Third World' became one of the most overworked terms in political discourse in the 1960s and 1970s. While for the newly decolonised States of Asia and Africa and the developing States of Latin America, it became a badge to be worn in a battle to claim a rightful place in the comity of nations, the Western world used it as a term of abuse to be hurled at the marginalised States of the international system.

It was Alfred Sauvy, a French economist and demographer, who is believed to have coined the term "Third World" in 1952. Sauvy of course had the Third Estate of pre-revolutionary France in mind. His definition of the term alluded to "social groups other than the most privileged groups of the day, the clergy and the nobility (the First and Second Estates, respectively").[1] In common usage the Third World became a term to describe the emerging States, regarded by many as qualitatively different from older countries of Europe and North America and certain others, the so-called 'First World' and the socialist countries of Eastern and Central Europe, known as the 'Second World". Mao Zedong sought to give the Third World an even more exclusive connotation. According to him, the two superpowers, the United States and the Soviet Union made up the First World, the other developed countries, the satellites of the super powers, formed the Second World and, with the exception of Japan the rest of Asia, Africa and Latin America constituted the Third World. Although China did participate in the first Afro-Asian conference held in Bandung in 1995, the Non-Aligned countries refused to accept China as part of the Third World.

Sauvy's phrase became popular and widely acceptable as it replaced earlier pejorative terms such as "backward areas", "underdeveloped countries", "societies in transition" and, as some UN documents put it, "peripheral countries". In 1940s, the poor and marginalised countries of Africa, Asia and Latin America were usually described as "backward".

By the 1950s the term "underdeveloped" replaced "backward" which implied the existence of a potential that could be realised. Initially, the term 'Third World" was "rejected by both the West (because it suggested that some countries were poor as a result of some other countries exploiting them to become rich) and the East (because it, implied a non-socialist alternative to capitalism).[2]

The term 'Third World' gradually became universally acceptable with both political and socio-economic connotations. While in political terms, it referred to countries which were on the margins of the bipolar world, the World Bank began to use the term to refer to the low-income countries. The term Third World gained wider currency and the politically non-aligned, economically developing and less industrialised nations of the world were being referred to as such.

However, an influential Commission headed by Willy Brandt in its report "*North-South: A Programme for Survival*" and the *South Commission* headed by Julius Nyerere rejected the term 'Third World" altogether. Instead, they preferred the term "South" to refer to the developing States and "North" to describe the industrialised countries. As *Report of the South Commission* put it, "largely bypassed by the benefits of prosperity and progress," the South exists "on the periphery of the developed countries of the North". It further said, "while most of the people of the North are affluent, most of the people of the South are poor; while the economies of the North are generally strong and resilient, those of the South are mostly weak and defenceless; while the countries in the North are, by and large, in control of their destinies, those of the South are very vulnerable to external factors and lacking in functional sovereignty".[3]

In the 1970s, several new terms came into common use. One such term was "developing nations" which sought to remove all implications of inferiority involved in the term 'Third World'. However, a distinction was also made between the "oil-producing" and non-oil-producing" nations. Some even used the term "newly industrialising" countries to refer to the relatively well off countries of Asia and Latin America. At present, the appellations "Third World countries", "less developed nations" and "developing countries" are commonly used interchangeably. The term "South" became fashionable for a while but an essentially geographic expression, which makes a distinction between two hemispheres eventually, lost its appeal. True, the "North" consists largely of affluent nations. But it also comprises countries north of the equator such as India and the rest of South Asia, the Southeast Asia, Caribbean and Central America. "Western" countries like Japan, Austria and New Zealand also belong to the geographical South.

Some analysts reject the term "Third World" outright. For example, C R Hensman maintains that the so-called Third World countries hardly share common values, interests and objectives. "The notion of an independent southern Third World", Hensman contends, "is a romantic one at best. It can be studied only as an idea, as a dream, as a myth, or as political speculation, and not as an historical, sociological and moral reality".[4] Other analysts seek to analyse the world in more unitary terms. Immanuuel Wallerstein, for example, asserts that there is a single world economy and that is capitalist. The three tiers of the world economy are core, periphery and semi-periphery.[5]

Some analysts have proclaimed the end of the Third World. Bayart, for instance, maintains that the Third World no longer exists.[6] If the Third World countries were largely defined by their relations with the superpowers during the Cold War, Bayart argues, they certainly have lost their raison d'être. At a time of integrating global economies and a near universal embrace of market economy, the Third World countries can no longer insist on playing victims of the bipolar world. In the 60s and 70s, protagonists of Third Worldism sought to romanticise struggles waged by "the wretched of the earth" and create an impression that only the developed countries were oppressors, ignoring the role of tyrannical regimes in many Third World countries. Political leaders too spoke and visualised as if the masses of the Third World would rise up and use the state to produce an egalitarian political order more compassionate than capitalism and less oppressive than communism. In the Latin American context, this belief in Third Worldism was given expression in different countries at different times — Argentina during

Peronism, Mexico under Luis Echeverria and Venezuela during the Carlos Andres Perez regime. Today, cynicism and indifference have replaced much of the optimism of the 60s and 70s.

The term 'Third World' may have its pitfalls and many countries may be wary of using it to describe themselves, but it hasn't outlived its analytical usefulness. In the absence of better and more apt alternatives, the present writer will use the term 'Third World' in this book. The term "developing countries" will also be used interchangeably. That the Third World countries are diverse and at varying stages of economic development is an acknowledged fact but as the South Commission put it, "in this diversity there is a basic unity" and that what these countries "have in common transcends their differences; it gives them a shared identity and a reason to work together for common objectives".[7]

II. The Third World and its Vision

Over four billion people, three quarters of all humanity live in the Third World. The primary engine of conflict in international politics may have changed from the East-West to the North-South divide, but the division between the First World and the Third World, despite globalisation, has only further widened. While few Third World countries have graduated into the First World, almost all countries of the Second World have joined the ranks of the developing world. According to Manfred Woechlcke of the Institute for Politics and Economics at Ebenhausen, Germany, of the 6 billion people on the planet by the turn of the century, 2 billion each will be poor and desperately poor.[8] Nearly four-fifths of the population will be living in the Third World.

The Third World countries share several common features. One such feature is their common colonial bondage of the past. While the Latin American States were decolonised in the early part of the 19th century following the two successful revolutions, the American (1776) and the French (1789) and the Napoleonic wars, particularly Napoleon's success in the Peninsular War(1807-14), Afro-Asian decolonisation was entirely a post-war phenomenon. The primary bond that linked Latin American States and the newly decolonised countries of Asia and Africa was their desire to escape from dehumanising poverty and underdevelopment and a yearning for a better quality of life for their citizens. It was this post-colonial surge of nationalism and the attendant emphasis on national sovereignty and self-reliance which became the hallmark of Third Worldism. Common problems of poverty, low productivity, population growth, unemployment, primary product export dependence and international vulnerability bonded them together in their demand for a just world economic order.

Largely bypassed by the modern industrial and technological advance thanks to the foreign rule and colonial politics, these countries developed prior to independence, as dependencies of economic, cultural and political centres elsewhere. They were at the dawn of their independence "unindustrialised, illiterate and characterised internally by extreme inequalities of wealth, influence and power between the people and an elite minority".[9]

The Third World assumed importance in the 60s and 70s for a variety of reasons. It had, and continues to have, enormous natural and human resources. It produces most of the world's oil and other raw materials. Without them, the industrial economies would collapse. The Third World countries embraced development in order to secure not only their independence from colonialism, but to meet rising expectations of material betterment. The experience was not very happy. In fact, it wouldn't be wrong to assume that the "revolution of rising expectations" was aborted even before it could take off. As proponents of the "dependency theory" argue, "the underdevelopment of the periphery is a condition of the development of the centre" and what happens at the end of the periphery is "the development of underdevelopment."[10]

The Third World became a cockpit of wars largely due to superpower rivalries. Poverty, malnutrition and disease, they say, are the ideal breeding grounds for political turmoil. Despair, despotism and cynical superpower opportunism all combined in the Third World to create a festering climate of economic collapse and political turmoil. As George Thomas Kurian says in the Preface of the *Encyclopedia of the Third World,* "the most significant political and social upheavals of modern time have occurred

The Third World in the Age of Globalisation:
Requiem or New Agenda?

Ash Narain Roy

Madhyam Books
Delhi

Zed Books
London & New York

global economic situation calling for a unified response from the Third World on development and trade. It was again due to the pressure from the Third World that the UN Development Decade was proclaimed. Between 1964 and 1970, the focus of the development debate shifted from the need for foreign aid to improving the access of Third World manufactures and semi-manufactured exports to Western markets.

It was at the special session of the UN General Assembly in 1974 where the demand for the establishment of NIEO was made. The Third World countries argued that nothing short of a complete re-structuring of the prevailing world order would provide an enduring solution to the world economic problems particularly those of the developing countries. The collapse of the post-war monetary system, emergence of restrictive and protectionist policies in the world market trade, recession, mounting inflation and, above all, the steadily deteriorating levels of real income from exports of primary produce were the inevitable consequences of the unjust world order. The developing world demanded a new order "based on equity, sovereign equality, interdependence, common interest and cooperation among all States"[14] In concrete terms, the Third World countries demanded through NIEO "non-discriminatory and preferential treatment for their manufactured goods in the markets of industrialised countries, more stable and higher prices for their commodities, renegotiations of their external public debt, codes of conduct for the activities of multinational corporations, more transfer of technology to less developed countries and a greater voice in the management of the world's monetary system."[15]

These demands required the active co-operation of the developed world. The Third World countries blamed the intransigent attitude of the developed world and their refusal to engage in serious negotiation to implement the Charter of Economic Rights and Duties of States and the Programme of Action on the Establishment of the New International Economic Order which prevented the fundamental restructuring of international economic relations. They also condemned the inflexible positions of most of the developed countries at the UNCTAD meetings which led to a further aggravation of the already deteriorated situation of international relations. Though the North-South summit took place at Cancun in 1981, major Western powers distanced themselves from the institutions and mores of multilateral diplomacy. The call to rekindle international concern for the plight of the Third World as contained in the Brandt report fell on deaf ears.

If there was little progress in North-South dialogue, South-South co-operation too ended up being "mere statements of pious platitudes and good intentions."[16] The Third World countries did make efforts to activate South-South co-operation and the New Delhi NAM Summit sought to inject a sense of urgency to the question. However, it was realised that unless the developing countries could organise and improve their bargaining power, their plans for restructuring the international economic system would not be taken seriously. At the Eighth NAM Summit at Havana, a South Commission was established under the chairmanship of Dr Julius Nyerere. An extraordinary ministerial conference of Non-Aligned countries on South-South co-operation was held in Pyongyang in 1987. Another meeting was held in Harare in 1989 for individual and collective self-reliance among the developing countries. The Ninth Summit of NAM further reaffirmed its determination to strengthen co-operation among NAM and other Third World countries. NAM leaders emphasised the need for streamlining South-South co-operation.

If the Thatcherite and Reaganian revolution of the 80s saw the developed world progressively retreating from the multilateral diplomacy, the disintegration of the Soviet Union, the end of Cold War and the advent of globalisation had profound implications for the Third World. It was at this stage the G-15, a representative, trans-regional group of countries with an umbilical chord to the other two movements of the South—the G-77 and NAM, was born. The G-15 promised to be more focused and action-oriented body unlike the G-77. It sought to build credibility through the successful implementation of projects for South-South co-operation and a non-confrontational, non-rhetorical but substantive dialogue with the North in a spirit of mutual benefit, shared responsibility and global partnership. The G-15 sought to make a break with the reflexive, recriminatory and self-righteous tone of previous

Preface

At the end of the millennium, the world seems to be facing paradigm shifts. Anxiety and disorientation are one result, but one also feels a sense of opportunity and hope. Can we detect an emerging global order in the trends of world economics and politics today? Can we successfully identify the underlying forces, the fundamental sources of change, which will shape events in the next century? After a century of global wars and nearly 50 years of Cold War, the world has entered an era when wars among the major powers seem a near impossibility despite NATO's barbaric air attacks against Yugoslavia; but wars among and within the smaller nation-states threaten to become even more intense than before.

The world is on the cusp of new ideological and economic paradigms. Every country in the world is being asked to fit the same model. If liberal democracy is the model which has found a near universal acceptability, the market-oriented economic reform is the new creed. Ironically, market economy is already in deep trouble in many places even if its triumph is proclaimed. If the economy fails, can democracy be a success?

Until recently, the primary engine of conflict in international politics was the East-West divide. Today, it is the North-South split. The development gap between the rich and poor nations has created a new duality in the world. The computer and digital highway represent the basis for a new industrial revolution to match those built on steam, the railways and the internal combustion engine. This is bound to cause dislocation all around just as previous periods of dramatic industrial change did.

Where does the Third World find itself in the emerging global order? Has the Third World ideology run out of steam? Are Non-Alignment and other Third Worldist ideologies the concepts whose time has passed? Is it the time to write an obituary of the Third World? What is the agenda before the Third World in the 21st century? This book makes an attempt to answer some of these questions.

III. Outline of the Book

For historic and geo-political reasons, Latin America has remained somewhat lukewarm towards NAM and other Third World fora. Latin America's interest in NAM and other Third World initiatives has waxed and waned according to the political character of the different regimes as also their foreign policy and domestic imperatives. Latin American States have been rightly described as the 'Achilles heel' of the Third World movement. They have often shown a proclivity to break ranks with the Third World if their perceived self-interests and Third World solidarity pose conflicting demands. Latin America's peripheral role in the Non-Aligned Movement is an illustrating case in point.

Is Latin America's relatively marginal role in NAM and other Third World fora the result of a widely held perception that it has very little in common with the rest of the developing world? Or is it the result of a realisation that their economic integration with the US is the surest route of upward mobility from the Third World to the First World? These questions have been often raised but hardly any systematic effort been made to analyse them. This book is not overburdened with theory. The endeavour is to carefully study and analyse explanatory paradigms to explain the Third World's increasing peripherisation and Latin America's marginal role in Third World politics. Detailed analysis of the region's peculiarities, its proximity to the northern behemoth, the United States, and its subdued role in the Non-Aligned Movement will enable us to appreciate and understand how Latin American foreign policy has developed in the past five decades.

Development studies have often been trapped in an overly dichotomised debate. Third World politics has been dominated largely by two broad schools of analysis, developmental and dependency theory. I have sought to critically analyse the available literature both in English and Spanish and hold extensive discussions with Latin American leaders, experts and diplomats to get useful insights into the full complexities and dynamics of Latin America's role vis-à-vis the Third World.

The book is divided into six broad chapters. Chapter I attempts, as we have already seen, an overview analysis of the evolution of Third World politics which provides an analytical framework for the subsequent chapters. Chapter II endeavours to analyse Latin America's peculiar traits which distinguish it from Asia and Africa. In Chapter III we discuss Latin America's unique ties with the US. Special attention is paid to how Latin America has traditionally looked on the US as a big, oppressive power and has defined its foreign policy primarily in opposition to the US and yet its manoeuvrability in international relations has been limited by the US' overbearing presence. Chapter IV deals with Latin America's role in the Non-Aligned Movement. Chapter V dwells at the emerging post-Cold War world order and its implications for world politics. The final chapter speculates on the options before the Third World countries in the context of the new world order.

Notes and References

1. Joel Krieger, (ed.), *The Oxford Companion to Politics of the World* (New York: Oxford University Press, 1993), pp. 908-909.

2. T J S George, (compiled), *The Enquire Dictionary: Ideas, Issues, Innovations*, (New Delhi: Harper-Collins, 1998), pp. 463-464.

3. See *The Challenge to the South: The Report of the South Commission*, (London, Oxford University Press, 1992), p. 1; Also see, *North-South: A Programme for Survival* (Cambridge: Mass 1980).

4. C R Hensman, *The Polemics of Revolt: From Gandhi to Guevara* (Allen Lane: Penguin 1969), p. 36.

5. Immanuel Wallerstein, cited in *The Oxford Companion to Politics of the World, Op. Cit.*, p. 909.

6. J F Bayart, "Finishing with the Idea of the Third World: The Concept of the Political Trajectory", in J Manor (ed.), *Rethinking Third World Politics* (Harlow, Longman, 1991), pp. 51-71; Also see M Berger, "The End of the Third World", *Third World Quarterly* Vol. 15, No. 2, 1994, pp. 257-75; and N Harris, *The End of the Third World* (London: Penguin, 1987).

X

their time and discussing a wide-range of issues pertaining to Latin America's role vis-à-vis the Third World. I am extremely thankful to Mexican Foreign Ministry for a 5-week invitation to lecture at El Colegio de Mexico and other universities in March 1999. I am grateful to Professor Issam El-Zaim of El Colegio de Mexico for his insightful comments on the future of the Third World.

I am specially grateful to Ms Purba Dutt whose comments on the first draft were stimulating and unfailingly sharp which enriched my understanding of the subject. Particular thanks are due to my wife Dina who constantly stood by me to make up for my inadequacy in the art of word processing. My 8-year-old daughter Martina kept reminding me of my progress all through the completion of this book. I am equally indebted to Mr Shelbi Joseph for his assistance in the preparation of this book in camera ready form. Particular thanks are due to Mr Kavaljit Singh of Madhyam Books and Robert Molteno of Zed Books for their keen interest in the book.

Finally, the debt I owe to my parents defies any description in words and for the fear of rendering it formal, I prefer to leave it at its source — the very depths of my inner self.

New Delhi   Ash Narain Roy

I

Introduction

Revolutionaries are usually the last people to grasp that they are past their sell - by date. Third Worldism, once a reigning ideology in much of the developing world is, today, in disarray, and Third World politics or 'Third World-ness' is adrift. The Non-Aligned Movement (NAM) was once a beacon for Third World countries in their fight for freedom, world peace, justice and human welfare. Presently, with the United States the only superpower left, and Russia still smarting from its dramatic loss of world power status, NAM and the protagonists of Third Worldism are scrambling to show they are not sitting pointlessly out on a limb.

The Third World politics is facing not just a mid-life but possibly a terminal crisis. It is no longer possible to look at world developments from the point of view of superpower rivalries today, for this paradigm has lost its relevance in the post-Cold War era. Whichever way one looks at the contemporary world, the realisation is gradually dawning on portrayals, and have often reinforced successive American Governments' political slant and agenda in the Latin American region. An impression has been created that Latin America is governed by moustachioed *caudillos* who gallop in and out of the presidential palace with sickening regularity. The other image is of poor and simpleton peasants with big sombreros either taking siestas under the palm trees or dancing gaily in the streets.

I. Smiling Mask

Given Latin America's peculiar history and colonial legacy and the predominance of authoritarianism and indigenous theocracies, it has developed a peculiar trait of remaining silent about its feelings and intentions but quite vocal about its appearances. Silence and appearance have historically been crucial tools for survival. The habits of keeping silent and maintaining appearances underlie the attitudes, opinions and behaviours, which are at the centre of the Latin American soul. Octavio Paz describes this attitude as a "smiling mask".[1] Such a trait has an important bearing on Latin America's role in the Third World fora, which we will see later in course of discussion. Latin America has also suffered from a serious identity crisis. Is it Western, non-Western, developing, Third World or neither? Or all? Simon Bolivar once asked: "If we are not Indians, nor Negroes, nor Europeans, who are we?" The answer is complex.

Though Latin Americans mostly consider themselves part of the Western culture, such characterisation is debatable. According to Wiarda and Kline, "with strong roots in Roman law, Catholicism and the Iberian socio-political tradition, Latin America is Western; yet it represents a particular Luso-Hispanic variant of the Western tradition and is obviously quite different in its social and cultural underpinnings from the variant established by the British in North America"[2] Urquidi, Sanchez and Terrazas support such a characterisation. As they maintain: "Latin America is a daughter of Western culture, with autochthonous pre-Colombian cultures and some aspects of African cultures added in varying proportions to different geographical areas".[3] Even Huntington considers Latin America largely as part of the Western culture.[4]

Latin American societies, according to one analyst, remain "heavily bifurcated and characterised by a European, wealthy elite in policy-making positions on one hand and a non-European, poor, marginalised population on the other."[5] The ethnic composition of Latin America too is diverse. If Argentina, Chile, Uruguay and Costa Rica are predominantly white and European, Andean countries like Peru, Ecuador and Bolivia, Central America and Mexico are mestizo, with a fairly high percentage of indigenous peoples. In Brazil, Cuba and the Dominican Republic, mulattos constitute an important segment of the population. A tradition of massive miscegenation is also unique. Mexico elected a recognisably Indian, Benito Juarez, as President as early as 1861. At the time of writing Argentina has as President a Syrian Muslim immigrant and Peru a Japanese immigrant. Both choices are still unthinkable in the US. Latin America also remains outside the vicious circle of ethnic politics or religious fundamentalism which ravages the other continents.

While some Latin American countries are fairly industrialised, others are a mix of the most backward areas and the most modern urban centres. The per capita income, literacy rates, urbanisation and other social indicators also show a remarkable variation. While Latin America's diversities must be recognised, its similarities too are striking especially when one compares them to other regions of Asia and Africa. Culturally, politically or otherwise, a common identity in Asia or 'Asian-ness' is totally non-existent. Though African States are often clubbed together in terms of their colonial experiences and other traits, they are too diverse to be treated as a single unit. Lusophone Africa is strikingly different from Francophone or Anglophone Africa. In the case of Latin America there are cogent reasons for treating the 20-odd States as a single culture area. As Wiarda and Kline maintain, "in their common Iberian colonial past, their institutional foundations, their struggles for independence, their cultural commonalties and continuities, and their often parallel development processes, the nations of Latin America have had some remarkably analogous experiences".[6]

By the 1950s the term "underdeveloped" replaced "backward" which implied the existence of a potential that could be realised. Initially, the term 'Third World" was "rejected by both the West (because it suggested that some countries were poor as a result of some other countries exploiting them to become rich) and the East (because it, implied a non-socialist alternative to capitalism).[2]

The term 'Third World' gradually became universally acceptable with both political and socio-economic connotations. While in political terms, it referred to countries which were on the margins of the bipolar world, the World Bank began to use the term to refer to the low-income countries. The term Third World gained wider currency and the politically non-aligned, economically developing and less industrialised nations of the world were being referred to as such.

However, an influential Commission headed by Willy Brandt in its report *"North-South: A Programme for Survival"* and the *South Commission* headed by Julius Nyerere rejected the term 'Third World" altogether. Instead, they preferred the term "South" to refer to the developing States and "North" to describe the industrialised countries. As *Report of the South Commission* put it, "largely bypassed by the benefits of prosperity and progress," the South exists "on the periphery of the developed countries of the North". It further said, "while most of the people of the North are affluent, most of the people of the South are poor; while the economies of the North are generally strong and resilient, those of the South are mostly weak and defenceless; while the countries in the North are, by and large, in control of their destinies, those of the South are very vulnerable to external factors and lacking in functional sovereignty".[3]

In the 1970s, several new terms came into common use. One such term was "developing nations" which sought to remove all implications of inferiority involved in the term 'Third World'. However, a distinction was also made between the "oil-producing" and non-oil-producing" nations. Some even used the term "newly industrialising" countries to refer to the relatively well off countries of Asia and Latin America. At present, the appellations "Third World countries", "less developed nations" and "developing countries" are commonly used interchangeably. The term "South" became fashionable for a while but an essentially geographic expression, which makes a distinction between two hemispheres eventually, lost its appeal. True, the "North" consists largely of affluent nations. But it also comprises countries north of the equator such as India and the rest of South Asia, the Southeast Asia, Caribbean and Central America. "Western" countries like Japan, Austria and New Zealand also belong to the geographical South.

Some analysts reject the term "Third World" outright. For example, C R Hensman maintains that the so-called Third World countries hardly share common values, interests and objectives. "The notion of an independent southern Third World", Hensman contends, "is a romantic one at best. It can be studied only as an idea, as a dream, as a myth, or as political speculation, and not as an historical, sociological and moral reality".[4] Other analysts seek to analyse the world in more unitary terms. Immanuuel Wallerstein, for example, asserts that there is a single world economy and that is capitalist. The three tiers of the world economy are core, periphery and semi-periphery.[5]

Some analysts have proclaimed the end of the Third World. Bayart, for instance, maintains that the Third World no longer exists.[6] If the Third World countries were largely defined by their relations with the superpowers during the Cold War, Bayart argues, they certainly have lost their raison d'être. At a time of integrating global economies and a near universal embrace of market economy, the Third World countries can no longer insist on playing victims of the bipolar world. In the 60s and 70s, protagonists of Third Worldism sought to romanticise struggles waged by "the wretched of the earth" and create an impression that only the developed countries were oppressors, ignoring the role of tyrannical regimes in many Third World countries. Political leaders too spoke and visualised as if the masses of the Third World would rise up and use the state to produce an egalitarian political order more compassionate than capitalism and less oppressive than communism. In the Latin American context, this belief in Third Worldism was given expression in different countries at different times — Argentina during to participate and by 1920, most of Latin America had joined the League of Nations. Two Latin Americans served as presidents of the Assembly; delegates from three Latin American countries presided over the Council, two jurists were among the seven Justices of the Permanent Court of International Justice at the Hague. There were neither African nor Asian participants in the Peace Conference. India and China were the only two founding members from Asia, and Liberia was the sole representative from Africa. Ethiopia and Egypt joined the League only later.

In Latin America the world wars and the global economic depressions of the 1930s combined to produce political effects different from those of Asia and Africa. While most Asian and African countries were facing the rigours of a brute colonial order, Latin American States increasingly aligned themselves with the US and Europe. Except for Argentina, which waited until the end of the Second World War, all other Latin American States followed the US lead. Brazil sent troops to Italy and Mexico provided bases and other military facilities to the US. Valuable raw materials flowed from Latin America into the war effort. Twenty-one Latin American States participated in the San Francisco Conference, that gave rise to the United Nations. The representation of Asia and Africa was rather meagre. In the initial years of the post - War period, those 21 votes, of an original 51 UN members, formed the nucleus of a Western bloc in the General Assembly and tilted the balance of power in favour of the Western camp. The Latin American countries thus knew which side of the Cold War division they were on.

At a time when the British, French, Dutch and other European powers were getting a firm hold in Asia and Africa or when they were at the apogee of their colonial hold, the decolonisation process was nearly underway in the Spanish and Portuguese colonies in Latin America. Beginning in the early 19th century, each successive period of international upheaval has resulted in a significant net accretion of States. The dismantling of the Spanish and Portuguese empires and the creation of several new States in Latin America and the Caribbean were the inevitable consequence of the Napoleonic wars. The second wave of creation of new States followed the World War I. The demise of the Ottoman Empire was a catalyst for the independence of a number of countries in West Asia and North Africa, including North Yemen, Egypt, Iraq and Oman. However, it was the Second World War, which sounded the death knell of nearly all colonial powers. The decolonisation process was nearly complete by the mid-60s except in the Caribbean and in certain pockets of Africa. A fourth wave of creation of new States came at the end of the Cold War. Scores of new States came into being following the disintegration of the Soviet Union and Yugoslavia. The Checz Republic and Slovakia fell apart following a velvet divorce. The African continent too saw the emergence of Namibia and Eritrea.

Latin America's decolonisation experience was unique in many ways. It was one of the most "internationalist" processes of independence. As Haynes says, "few Third World States in modern times gained their independence from colonial control by way of a unifying liberation war unlike, for example, the United States' fight for freedom from Britain in the late eighteenth century or Latin American States' struggle for independence from Spanish or Portuguese control in the early nineteenth century."[9] In fact, Manuel Perez Guerrero goes to the extent of arguing that Simon Bolivar's vision, particularly his "universal project for the political emancipation of Latin America" laid the foundation for the modern-day "Third Worldist cause".[10] Simon Bolivar is revered in Latin America as the liberator of five Latin American countries: Bolivia, Colombia, Ecuador, Peru and Venezuela.

In the field of international relations, Bolivar proposed the extension of the "balance of power" idea to the entire world. Originally it referred to a balance in Europe. He supported a balance composed of the Americans on one side and most of Europe on the other. This balance when held in equilibrium, Bolivar believed, would maintain the independence of South America. To keep this balance England should ally itself with the Spanish-American countries. The world balance, Bolivar contended, should be a factor in Latin American policy.[11] In 1826 Bolivar convened the Congress of Panama with a view to providing the basis for what he called "a league of poor nations", which would serve as a counterweight to the military alliances of the time and a bulwark against colonialism and foreign domination.

So long as Latin America formed part of the Spanish Empire, it was as though it did not exist on the international plane. Spain set out to construct a series of legal and cultural barriers to disguise and even destroy the seeming Latin American unity the colonial power did not want its subjects to perceive. For example the Spaniards tried to impose a strict quarantine on the whole of the New World, by making access difficult for foreigners. Even the inhabitants were forbidden to move from one province to another without royal permission. The *Leyes de Indias* forbade trade with foreigners, under any pretext. Bolivar fought against this and sought to inculcate universalist vision among the Latin Americans. Bolivar sought the unity of Latin America. He believed that "America could communicate its revolutionary fervour to Africa and Asia, and destroy the yoke of servitude that Europe at this period had hung upon the rest of the world."[12] Bolivar aimed at continental federation which would have a unified foreign policy and mutual co-operation in internal defence.

Thus Latin America's struggle for political independence, long before that of Asia and Africa, highlighted human freedom, state sovereignty and self-determination. According to Aristides Royo, former President of Panama, "the historical continuity that exists between the liberator's (Bolivar's) concepts and proposals and the essence of the Non-Aligned Movement, is ....obvious. And this explains why the non-aligned policy, with its resolute opposition to all forms and manifestations of foreign domination, whether of the imperialist, colonialist, neo-colonialist, racist or apartheid regime type is in full accord with Bolivar's concept".[13] It is interesting to note that at a time when the United States was propounding the much-maligned "Monroe Doctrine", Bolivar convened the Congress of Panama where he propounded a principle of Latin American solidarity and rejected the politics of hegemonism. As Demetrio Boersner maintains, "while the essence of Monroe was fundamentally hegemonist which reflected the expansionist ambitions of the dominant sections of the US, Bolivar's scheme was internationalist and democratic".[14]

Ironically, the new rulers abandoned the Bolivarian vision in the post-independence era. During the independence wars Latin American patriots tried to imitate the republics of Europe by imitating their constitutions and laws. However, when the time came to apply those constitutions to a people who had no democratic tradition whatsoever, the efforts failed. Very quickly, Latin America had the *caudillos* once again. Revolutions too merely succeeded in replacing one *caudillo* with another. Latin America was also caught in the expanding vortex of the internationalist capitalist system. Its economy was shaped by the needs of the Western capitalist centres. Latin America saw the emergence of an alliance between the oligarchy and the military. The comprador elites did all that the conquistadors had done during the colonial era. As exporters of a limited number of primary products the Latin American economy, while responding to the international market forces, developed the distortions of dependent capitalism.

We have seen how Latin America's decolonisation experience was different from Asia and Africa. We have also seen how by the 1920s Latin America was well integrated into the Western camp. By the time newly emerging Asian and African countries began to forge their independent identity in world politics and chose not to join either the capitalist camp or the communist camp, Latin American countries already had 130 to 150 years of independent life, bereft of any alignments behind them. By virtually any criterion, almost all the Latin American nations were more developed than the Third World nations of Asia and Africa. They were, thus, not comfortable being lumped together with other Third World nations. If at all, many thought they had better credentials to lead the Third World than Asia and Africa.

Latin America had certain other advantages over Africa and Asia. First, the concepts of nation and of state were much more firmly rooted in Latin America than elsewhere in the Third World. Second, Latin America was more industrialised than the other two continents. It had longer exposure to the utilisation of modern technology. The levels of infrastructural development and urbanisation were also much higher than the rest of the Third World. Latin America also had better pragmatic international co-operation programmes than did Asia and Africa. Urquidi, Sanchez and Terrazas called it "Bolivar's inspirational ideal of continental unity"[15] which saw the emergence of regional integration bodies like the *Asociacion Latino-Americana de Libre Comercio* (ALAC), Latin American Free Trade Association (LAFTA), the Andean Pact, the Central American Common Market, the Amazon Pact and so on. Latin America's experience at regional integration will be discussed at length later.

There is another reason why Latin America remained somewhat aloof from NAM and Third World initiatives. Unlike Asia and Africa, there has been no sharp distinction between foreign and domestic policy in the Latin American countries. International relations are regarded as a means of attaining various domestic objectives or, more correctly, a means of attaining objectives that are categorised as neither foreign nor domestic, but simply as national objectives – especially national economic objectives. Take the case of Brazil. The Brazilian foreign policy is generally viewed in terms of its possible contribution to internal economic development. It was more so during the "miracle" years. As J P dos Reis Velloso, the then Planning Minister said in 1972, Brazilian national interest in the field of international policy lay in conducting foreign relations "in consonance with the national development strategy, orienting them to the objective of the most rapid growth, modernisation and greater competitive power of the national economy."[16] Rather than pursuing an activist foreign policy through NAM or Third World fora Brazilian leaders visualised that once its internal development progress and the economic strength were increasingly recognised as such abroad, Brazil's international prestige would rise concomitantly.

On this count, it would appear that what is true of Brazil is also largely true of the other countries in the region. Mexico's international policy too has had somewhat similar objectives, though its role at times varied with the priorities of different regimes. Mexico's foreign policy has been determined traditionally by two main factors. The first is the active utilisation of actions abroad "as an element of legitimisation and counterbalance to the political system within the country". The second factor is the use of its global foreign policy stance "as an element to counterbalance what is the most important tie that Mexico has with a foreign country, its relations with the United States.[17]

The Latin American countries are a very diverse collection of States, differing in many ways that influence directly or indirectly both foreign policy and international behaviour. These include level of economic development, degree of political development, historical experiences in the international arena, political ideology, skills and perceptions of political leaders, political and economic resources, to name a few. Security and survival and economic development, not so much a high profile and ideologically-inspired, independent status in the international system, have been the primary goals of foreign policy. It should be noted here that while foreign policy objectives of Latin American countries seem identical, or at least very similar, policies and approaches have not always been the same.

III. Oligarchy, the Military and Revolution

Reasons for Latin America's inward policy in foreign affairs or its excessive dependence on the United States are not hard to find. As Demetrio Boersner persuasively argues, Latin America since its colonial days has been subjected continuously to "certain forms of external domination: colonial during the period prior to independence; semi-colonial during the 19th century and till the end of the Second World War; and neo-colonial form 1945 onwards".[18] The political history of independent Latin America exhibited a strong element of continuity with the colonial past. Post-colonial political and economic elites were the same people of European stock as dominated during the colonial era. The post-independence period saw the rise of *caudillismo*, which was a highly personalised form of government. The economic system that Latin America developed during that period owed its origins to European influences.

In the 1920s, when economic depression caused a number of political and economic upheavals, the State in Latin America which represented the interest of raw materials exporters and large landowners, protected the interests of that very class. Just as the landed elites and merchants who exported Latin America's wealth pursued their interests in maintaining dependent economic patterns, the modern industrial managers and military elites favoured foreign interests. They also feared the demands of the masses, preferring military dictatorship to nationalistic reform or revolution. Import substituting for industrialisation did not create a basis for sustained growth. The industrial bourgeoisie was transformed into an agent of foreign capital, playing a functional role similar to that of the agro-commerical elites, which it had joined or defeated.

In the post-War period, when newer and newer States in Asia and Africa emerged on the scene, Latin America took some tentative steps towards democratisation. In the 1940s, democratic elections were held in Guatemala, Venezuela and Costa Rica. These democracies, however "died in infancy; by the early 1950s, Venezuela and Guatemala were again military dictatorships"[19] The increasing industrialisation and urbanisation combined to generate strong popular pressures for increased social spending and greater political participation. But what followed was not more democracy but authoritarianism. The second wave of democratisation began in 1955. By 1960, only Paraguay in all of South America had a dictator at the helm. Then again followed a spate of coups. By mid-70s elected civilian governments survived only in Colombia, Venezuela and Costa Rica.

The military regimes in Latin America with some exceptions promoted the interest and economic domination of a small, exclusivist group whose chief loyalty was to itself rather than to the nation. This oligarchy sought to exclude the mass of people from political decision-making by banning elections and by directing state spending to areas to build up infrastructure attractive to foreign capital and to state bureaucracy, especially the military. In foreign relations, these regimes cultivated ties with Western industrialised powers, especially the United States. Their main objectives were "attracting foreign investment and aid, implementing a neoliberal economic model, avoiding active participation in overly Third-World-oriented multilateral organisations such as the Non-Aligned Movement, the Organisation of Petroleum Exporting Countries (OPEC) and the UN Conference on Trade and Development (UNCTAD), and paying particular attention to foreign-policy questions important to the USA, such as illicit drug trafficking and immigration".[20]

The role of the military regimes in Brazil was radically different. Military officers overthrew the empire of Brazil, the only hereditary constitutional monarchy in Latin America, in 1887 and replaced it with a republic; then they conspired with Getulio Vargas to carry out the revolution of 1930; they worked with Vargas to establish the *estado novo* in 1937 and put an end to the populist regime of Joao Goulart in 1964. After taking power, the Brazilian military turned its back on the *caudillo* system prevalent in Spanish-American dictatorships. Although in sharp contrast to its earlier role as moderator of a political game, the military, from 1964 onwards, assumed the role of the director of the political system. While Brazilian foreign policy in the 1950s and upto 1964 was oriented to maximise national influence in international politics and to play an increasingly active role in world affairs, the decade following the 1964 Revolution was dedicated to the twin goals of economic growth and political stability. After 1964, Brazil's participation in the Third World fora continued, although with less stridency. Strong ties with Africa were established but such a policy was more historical and cultural than political and economic.

What, however, changed the course of Latin American foreign policy was the advent of the 1959 Cuban Revolution. In the aftermath of the overthrow of the Fulgencio Batista regime, Cuba underwent a dramatic change from an acquiescent client state of the United States to a defiantly independent actor in international politics under the leadership of Fidel Castro. Cuba was able to play an unprecedentedly important role in world affairs, somewhat disproportionate with the traditional attributes of power. What is, however, "novel about the Cuban example is that "its impact remained neither transitory nor ephemeral". Despite its small size, limited resource endowments, economic backwardness and other constraints, Cuba proved its capability to exercise influence far beyond its national frontiers".[21]

Between the Bandung conference of 1955 which was attended by 29 Afro-Asian States and was regarded as a historic occasion because it rallied Third World leaders on their own terms for the first time and the 1961 Begrade Summit of NAM, at least two dozen countries were decolonised. Some of them leaned far to the Left and many others became rather vocal in their anti-imperialist pronouncements. Thus, when Castro emerged on the world scene in the face of unremitting pressure from the US, the Cuban leader was assured of at least moral support from the non-aligned and other Third World countries. However, since the US assumed a moral role of combating communism, "Latin American nations were drawn into the Cold War as allies of the US in hemispheric solidarity against extra-continental threat from the Soviet Union".[22]

IV. Regional Economic Integration

There are no two opinions about the fact that Latin America has remained somewhat disinclined to play an activist role in the Non-Aligned Movement or other Third World fora for reasons discussed in the preceding pages. However, Latin America's key role in formulating schemes for meaningful co-operation among the Third World countries, particularly regional economic integration is universally recognised. If Latin American scholars like Prebisch, Furtado, Dos Santos, Cardoso etc contributed more than Asian or African writers to the development of the dependency theory, regarded as Latin America's major contribution to the social sciences, the economic integration process that began in Latin America in the 60s provided a model for other developing countries to emulate. It was Latin America's concern about their excessive dependence on the United States that these countries began to direct their efforts to co-ordinate the development and growth of their national economies through the establishment of regional and sub-regional associations. These experiments have included the Latin American Free Trade Association (LAFTA), the Andean Pact, Central American Common Market (CACM), the Caribbean Common Market (CARICOM) and the Southern Cone Group (CONOSUR).[23]

It was the United Nations Economic Commission for Latin America (ECLA) which developed the concept of regional economic co-operation modelled on West European experience of free trade. ECLA believed that integration measures like liberalisation of international trade, adoption of a common tariff for member countries of a regional body and the co-ordination of investment policies theoretically would make the regionalisation of import substitution policies more viable. The underlying principle for such an experiment was greater strength through organisation. Two such regional organisations, LAFTA and CACM were created thanks to the ECLA proposals. Founded in 1960 through the Treaty of Montevideo, by Argentina, Brazil, Chile, Paraguay, Peru and Uruguay, LAFTA was later joined by Colombia, Ecuador, Venezuela and Bolivia. The CACM was established by the Treaty of Managua in 1961 by Costa Rica, El Salvador, Guatemala, Honduras and Nicaragua. The main objectives of CACM were the eventual elimination of all tariffs and barriers between members and the establishment of a common external tariff for the rest of the world, a common customs administration, unified fiscal policy and co-ordinated regional policies in public health, labour, education, transport and agriculture.

These two integration efforts were largely unsuccessful. The disparate size and levels of economic development of member countries created significant obstacles to economic integration. Argentina, Brazil and Mexico benefited disproportionately from intra-zonal trade. According to Milenky, the failure of LAFTA and CACM to promote economic integration was primarily due to shifting ideologies towards development through central state planning "rather than reliance on private enterprise or a more open economic setting and complete structures of industry over a share in a regional market".[24]

The Andean pact was a consequence of, in part, as a reaction and growing resentment against big countries' clout in LAFTA. Bolivia,

Colombia, Chile, Ecuador and Peru, who were dissatisfied with the distribution of benefits with LAFTA and felt their progress would be smoother in a group that excluded Brazil and Argentina, formed the Andean Pact. This pact marked a move away from the integration process based on the European model. As Lynn Mytelka argues, in order to be successful, integration schemes in lesser developed countries must include strategies to redistribute resources within the group as well as strategies to reduce dependence on external powers.[25] The Andean Pact sought to incorporate these strategies into its decisions and activities. The agreement creating the Andean Pact was perhaps the most innovative and far-reaching effort to establish a regional integration scheme in the Third World. It called for the establishment of a common external tariff, joint industrial programming, rapid creation of a free trade zone, harmonisation of economic and social priorities, common treatment of foreign investment and other programmes.

The Andean Pact too faced problems similar to other regional groupings. Chile withdrew from the pact in 1976 and dramatic changes in the sub-region and external processes hampered the growth of the Andean Common Market. The Andean pact was revitalised in 1988. Though intra-bloc trade increased significantly, drug problems and problems of terrorism in Colombia and Peru have come in the way of the Andean Pact realising its full potential. Latin America also saw the emergence of other sub-regional groups in the 1970s like the Plata Basin Group to develop international water resources and hydroelectric power, the Amazon Pact and the Latin American Energy Organisation (OLADE).

Perhaps the most ambitious and successful experiment in regional economic integration is the establishment of the *Mercado Comun del Sur* (MERCOSUR), the Common Market of the South. It is a only major customs union outside Europe. It was created in 1991 under the Treaty of Asuncion by Argentina, Brazil, Uruguay and Paraguay. MERCOSUR has a combined population of nearly 200 million, a total GDP of over $800 billion and trade (in either direction) of over $70 billion per year.Today it produces annually about US$420 billion worth of goods and services. The main objective of the regional grouping is free circulation of goods, services, capital and manpower. Despite its name, MERCOSUR is still some way from being a common market because free movement of labour remains a distant and difficult prospect. But it has come a long way. Most trade within MERCOSUR is already tariff-free, although free trade in all products will not be realised until 2000. A common external tariff has also been adopted on most products. However, the group will not become a full customs union until 2006.[26]

MERCOSUR has also widened its scope. Chile acceded in October 1996 as an associate member. It is part of the group's free trade zone without adopting the common external tariff. Bolivia, a member of the Andean Pact, negotiated a similar association in December 1996. Negotiations for a free association with other members of the Adean group – Colombia, Ecuador, Peru and Venezuela have also been held. MERCOSUR also signed an agreement with the European Union in 1995 to establish the model for negotiation of a trade pact. The free trade agreement between MERCOSUR and the EU is likely to be signed in 1999. As Manuel Marin, EU Commissioner responsible for relations with Latin America, says, "This will be the first time in the world that we put on the table liberalisation between one region and another".[27] If the trade deal materialises in 1999, it would start well before the 34-nation hemispheric free-trade zone-known as the Free Trade Area of the Americas (FTAA) by 2005. Since 1991, trade within MERCOSUR has grown rapidly – at an average 27 per cent a year from 1990 to 1995. It has risen five-fold to some $20 billion a year. One fifth of the four countries' foreign trade is now conducted with the other three MERCOSUR members, compared with 9 per cent in 1990. Trade between Brazil and Argentina has quadrupled since 1990 to more than $15 billion.

A bold and imaginative step towards meaningful regional economic integration came under the framework of the *Sistema Economico Latinoamericana* (SELA). Designed to co-ordinate Latin American strategy to regional and global problems, SELA was established at the initiative of Mexican President Luis Echeverria and President Carlos

Andres Perez of Venezuela. The two leaders were great votaries of Third Worldism. The initiative was based on the assumption that Latin American States would be more influential in the international system if they adopted common positions and regional unity towards the rest of the world. The SELA was of course not an economic integration scheme. It was mainly responsible for formulating Latin America's positions on economic questions both within and without the hemisphere.

The objective of SELA was to create and promote Latin American multinational enterprises; to protect the prices of basic commodities, while ensuring markets for exports from the region and to reinforce technological and scientific co-operation among member states.[28] These enterprises were to take on the most urgent needs of the SELA members in the case of production and services in the line of increasing their links. Perez and Echeverria also stressed the definition of a common position of the Latin American bloc in the main international meetings. With this in view, the rapid creation of the Multinational Shipping of the Caribbean (NAMUCAR) constituted an important landmark in fulfilling the objectives thus established. However, difficulties were not long in coming and were evident, especially in the apathy of the South American countries, which lowered the level of their representation in subsequent meetings. When President Lopez Portillo assumed office in Mexico in 1976, and his Government did not put as much emphasis on the tasks set out by his predecessor, the initial dynamism of the SELA flagged even further.

The SELA could not of course become a catalyst for co-ordinated regional action as its proponents had hoped, but it did develop a number of far-reaching projects that bespoke its seriousness in tackling developmental problems. As William A Hazelton says, SELA may have been plagued by internal squabbles and divergent policy perspectives but it provided "a link between Latin America and the Third World"[29] More than any other regions of the Third World, Latin America has been able to devise a coherent and recognisable body of literature about its economic needs; to relate them to internal co-ordination; and place them in a broader, international context. While that capacity has not led necessarily to greater effectiveness, it has nevertheless permitted the growth of a common understanding among governmental elites about the desirability, strength as well as the limitations of international discussion to resolve policy disputes.

V. Peaceful Vocation

Latin America has cultivated a unique cultural and diplomatic tradition that emphasises peaceful and diplomatic solution of conflicts and adherence to international laws and treaties. Regional peace initiatives of the 1980s to resolve the Central American crisis, was in keeping with that tradition. Known as the Contadora Initiative, Mexico, Venezuela, Panama and Colombia played an important role in formulating a regional framework to end the crisis. Foreign Ministers of the four countries met in the Contadora Island in Panama and discussed at length the critical situation prevailing in the region. In July 1983, the group held a summit meeting in Cancun, Mexico where the "Cancun Declaration" was issued. It called for the initiation of bilateral as well as regional negotiations among the Central American countires on the basis of an 8-point agenda: armament race in Central America; control and reduction of arms; arms traffic; presence of advisers or other forms of external military assistance; action designed to destabilise the internal order of other States; verbal threats or aggression; belligerent incidents and border tension; and grave problems of economic and social order as also questions of human rights.

The Contadora initiative received the backing of a large number of Latin American nations. In 1986, it issued the 'Declaration of Caraballeda' named after the Venezuelan resort, where it was signed by Contadora Foreign Ministers and their counterparts from the 'Support Group"(Argentina, Brazil, Peru and Uruguay). Earlier the group had prepared the Contadora draft treaty to be signed by all five Central American countries. It advocated a mutual reduction in arms, troops and foreign advisers throughout the region and the establishment of fair judicial systems and the guarantee of civil liberties, including free elections.[30] It was the ground prepared by the Contadora group which helped Costa Rican President Oscar Arias to propose a peace plan for Central America and to help end the danger of a regional war which won him the Nobel Peace Prize in the late 1980s.

Arias's idea was that Central America should try to solve their own problems, and persuade the superpowers to stand back. Arias spoke bluntly to Nicaragua's Sandinistas, so the US had to take him seriously. He also attacked Reagan's attempt to get rid of the Sandinistas, so nobody could call him a stooge of the Yankees. Having thus earned both criticism and a new respect, Arias sought backing for his plan from democracies outside the region. He was ensured of the Western world's support, at least, when the Nobel Committee gave him its peace prize. After much scepticism and many twists and turns, Arias Plan led to the ending of US military aid for the contras and the free election in Nicaragua.

In December 1986, eight foreign ministers of the Contadora and Support Group met in Rio de Janeiro and adopted a declaration creating the Permanent Mechanism of Consultation and Political Co-ordination, known as the Rio Group or the Group of Eight (G-8). The declaration provided for regular meetings of foreign ministers on topics of common interest. In addition, annual meetings of heads of state were begun in November 1987, and regular conferences of finance ministers were instituted the following year. Venezuelan President Carlos Andrez Perez told a meeting of the Organisation of American States (OAS) in 1990 that "the OAS has exhausted its role" and that there was need to "rethink the OAS and close the gap that has separated the North American vision of peace and security from the vision of the peoples of Latin America".[31] In 1991, the OAS approved the "Santiago Commitment to Democracy" which defined the general principle of representative democracy as a hemispheric goal, and it mandated the OAS to meet in the event of a coup against a democracy.

Another peculiar feature of Latin America that merits attention is the relative peace that it has enjoyed since the Chaco war of 1932-35 between Bolivia and Paraguay. There have, of course, been minor border conflicts between Peru and Ecuador, Chile and Argentina and the 1982 war between Argentina and Britain over the Malvinas, but compared to other parts of Third World, Latin America has been extraordinarily peaceful. Rarely have Latin American States used force to settle border disputes. The few wars that have been fought in the past 50 years have usually ended quickly. The most prolonged and costly wars since 1945 have not been between States but within them. For example, in Guatemala, it took 35 years and 100,000 deaths before any serious bid was made to end the civil war. In El Salvador, it took a dozen years and 75,000 lives before the peace accord could be signed in the early 1990s.

Latin America is also justifiably proud of the Tlatelolco Treaty, which bans nuclear weapons. It even preceded the Nuclear Non-Proliferation Treaty. Latin America is the first region in the world to sign a Treaty for the Prohibition of Nuclear Weapons, better known as the Tlatelolco Treaty way back in 1967, declaring the region as nuclear free. (The oldest treaty, technically speaking, was signed in 1959, which banned all nuclear weapons in the Antarctic). All Latin American and Caribbean States have made a commitment not to test, use, manufacture, produce or acquire nuclear weapons. Latin America has also created a regional organisation to ensure compliance with the Tlatelolco Treaty, the Agency for the Prohibition of Nuclear weapons in the region, which is known by its Spanish acronym OPANAL. A protocol commits States to respect the denuclearisation of Latin America and not to use or threat the use of nuclear weapons against any party. It was the intensive work in favour of disarmament that brought the Mexican Foreign Minister Alfonso Garcia Robles the Nobel Prize for Peace in 1982.

VI. Theology of Liberation

Catholicism has been enmeshed in Latin American politics from the days of the conquest by Spain and Portugal. The conquest itself was the result of joint efforts by the Church and the State. The Church has long been acknowledged as the bastion of conservatism in politics and a pillar of traditional order. For centuries the relation between Church and State was in terms of two powers—the spiritual and the temporal. Conflicts arose out of a tussle for supremacy. In the Latin American context the conflicts between the Church and the State were related to the more fundamental issue of understanding the nature of the Church itself and its relation to the world.

The theology of liberation, that explicitly rejected the Church's historical alliance with elites and repressive governments and declared the Church's preferential option for the poor, assumed a uniquely Latin American dimension. The 1968 Medellin Conference was a turning point in the history of the Latin American Church. It initiated new and far reaching changes in the realm of theological thought. Medellin did not create "liberation theology", neither did it formally endorse it – only on four occasions did the 'conclusions' arrived at used the term 'liberation'.[32]

As Jose Comblin, the theologian who assisted the Brazilian bishops at Medellin, says, the central theme of Medellin was liberation. The encouragement liberation theology received from Medellin contributed in no small measure to the plentiful and bold writings in the field of liberation theology. Christian revolutionaries like Camilo Torres related their revolutionary commitment to their Christian faith. They argued that political action for a profound social transformation was a necessary concomitant, even constituent of Christian faith – both laity and clergy. They also called upon Christians to act in alliance with any group (Marxists included) seeking change.

Liberation theology put the problems of overcoming poverty at the heart of Christian theology—instead of the problems of 'belief' that had preoccupied theology since Renaissance. Liberation theology altered the political and religious landscape of Latin America in the 1960s and 1970s. For liberation theology, Father Gustavo Gutierrez, a Peruvian priest viewed as the founding father of liberation theology, says, everything begins with the question, "How do you say to the poor, the oppressed, the insignificant person, God loves you?"

The liberation theology inspired thousands of priests, nuns and lay workers to take up life in shantytowns and villages. It also challenged long-standing links between the Roman Catholic Church and Latin American elites. The proponents of radical theology became victims of death squads but their commitments remained unchanged. Liberation theology still swears by some of its major themes but it has also followed the shift of Latin American social scientists away from "dependency theory".

In conclusion, Latin America's somewhat ambiguous and less committal role in Third World affairs is the result of its distinct tradition in colonisation, settlement and independence, social and political dynamics, and, above all, the factors that shaped its "special" ties with the United States under the broad framework of the Monroe Doctrine of the 19th century and the post-war Inter-American system. In terms of economic performance, social development, cultural homogeneity and strong diplomatic tradition, Latin America stands apart from Asia and Africa. That distinction provided ample opportunities for leadership of the Third World. But the region either squandered that opportunity to be a bigger player in the international system or it simply refused to believe that its future was linked inextricably to the rest of the Third World. The history of Third World will perhaps prove that Latin American countries often disowned their Third World identity when things did not go their way.

Notes and References

1. Octavio Paz, *The Labyrinth of Solitude: Life and Thought in Mexico* (New York: Grove, 1960), p. 29.

2. Howard J Wiarda and Harvey F Kline, *Latin American Politics and Development* (University of Massachusetts, 1979), p. 3.

3. Victor L. Urquidi, Vincente Sanchez and Eduardo Terrazas, "Latin America and World Problems: Prospects and Alternatives", in *Journal of Interamerican Studies and World Affairs,* Vol. 24, No. 1, February 1982, p. 14.

4. Samuel P. Huntington, *The Third Wave: Democratisation in the Late Twentieth Century* (Norman: University of Oklahoma Press, 1991), p. 299.

5. Jeanne A K Hey, "Three Building Blocks of a Theory of Latin American Foreign Policy", *Third World Quarterly*, Vol. 118, No. 4, 1997, p. 663.

6. Wiarda and Kline, *Op. Cit.*, p. 5.

7. Stanley J and Barbara H Stein, *The Colonial Heritage of Latin America* (New York: Oxford University Press, 1970), p. VII.

8. *Ibid.*

9. Jeff Haynes, *Third World Politics: A Concise Introduction* (Blackwell: Oxford, 1996), p. 28.

10. See *Manuel Perez Guerrero en l a Escena Internacional, Fundacion Biblioteca de Politica Exterior,* Ministerio de Relaciones Exteriores (Caracas, 1989), p. 41.

11. *Gazeta de Caracas,* 6 January 1814, as cited in J L Salcedo-Bastardo, ed, and trans by Annella McDermott, *Bolivar: A Continent and its Destiny* (The Richmond Publishing Co. Ltd, 1977), p. 89. Also see, Gerald E Fitzgerald, *The Political Thought of Bolivar: Selected Writings* (The Hague: Martinus Nijhoff,1971).

12. J.L Salcedo-Bastardo, *Op. Cit.,* p. 101.

13. See Aristides Royo's speech at NAM Summit in Havana, in *Addresses: Sixth Conference of Heads of State or Government of Non-Aligned Countries* (Havana; Editorial de Ciencias Sociales, 1980), p. 584.

14. Demetrio Boersner, *Relaciones Internacionales de America Latina* (Caracas: Editorial Nueva Sociedad, 1990), p. 122.

15. Victor L Urquidi, Vincente Sanchez and Eduardo Terrazas, *Op. Cit.,* p. 19.

16. J P dos Reis Velloso, cited in Norman A Bailey and Ronald M Schneider, "Brazil's Foreign Policy: A Case Study in Upward Mobility", *Inter-American Affairs,* Vol. 27, No. 4, Spring 1974, pp. 9-10.

17. Luis Maira, "Caribbean State Systems and Middle-Status Powers: The Cases of Mexico, Venezuela and Cuba" in Paget Henry and Carl Stone (eds.) *The Newer Caribbean: Decolonisation, Democracy and Development* (Philadelphia: Institute for the Study of Human Issues, 1983), p. 191.

18. Demetrio Boersner, *Op. Cit.,* p. 16.

19. Ash Narain Roy, "Democracy in Latin America" *Hispanistica* (New Delhi), Vol. I, No. 2, July 1993, p. 73.

20. Jeanne A K Hey, *Op. Cit.,* p. 7634.

21. Ash Narain Roy, *Cuba's Relations with the Soviet Union, 1968-1980,* Doctoral Thesis, Jawaharlal Nehru University, 1986, p. 1.

22. Jennie K Lincoln, "Introduction to Latin American Foreign Policy: Global and Regional Dimensions", in Elizabeth G Ferris and Jennie K Lincoln, (eds.), *Latin American Foreign Policies: Global and Regional Dimensions* (Boulder: Westview Press, 1981), p. 8.

23. For a detailed analysis of Latin America's regional economic integration, see Miguel S Wionczek, "The Rise and Decline of Latin American Economic Integration", pp. 506-521, in Yale Ferguson (ed), *Contemporary Inter-American Relations* (Englewood Cliffs, New Jersey, Prentice-Hall, 1972). Also see, Michel Teubal, "The failure of

Latin America's Economic Integration", pp. 120-144 in James Petras and Maurice Zeitlin, (eds), *Latin America: Reform or Revolution* (Greenwich, Connecticut, Fawcett Publications, 1968).

24. Edward S Milenky, "Latin America's Multilateral Diplomacy: Integration, Disintegration and Interdependence", *International Affairs*, Vol. 53, No.1, January 1977, p. 75.

25. Lynn Krieger Mytelka, *Regional Development in a Global Economy: The Multinational Corporation, Technology and Andean Integration* (New Haven: Yale University Press, 1979).

26. See "America Latina Comienza a Madurar", *El Mercurio* (Santiago), January 2, 1997. Also see "Derribando Fronteras", in the Economia y Negocios section of *El Mercurio,* July 31, 1996, pp. 30-31.

27. *Financial Times* (London), September 16, 1997.

28. George Thomas Kurian, *Encyclopaedia of the Third World* (London: Mansell Publishing Limited, 1982), p. 10.

29. William A Hazelton, "Will There Always be a Uruguay?: Interdependence and Independence in the Inter-American System", in Elizabeth G Ferris and Jennie K Lincoln, *Op. Cit.,* p. 77.

30. A N Roy, "Contadora Back in Saddle", *Link* (New Delhi), June 1, 1986. Also see Ash Narain Roy and Norma A Ramirez, "Contadora Peace Initiative: A Viable Alternative?", *National Herald* (New Delhi), December 19, 1983.

31. Robert A Pastor, " The Latin American Option", *Foreign Policy,* No. 88, Fall 1992, p. 111.

32. For detailed analysis of liberation theology, see Gustavo Gutierrez, *A Theology of Liberation* (New York: Meryknoll, Orbis Books, 1979); Alain Gheerbrant, *The Rebel Church in Latin America* (Harmondaworth: Penguin Books, 1974) and Juan Luis Segundo, *The Liberation of Theology* (New York: Orbis Books, 1976).

3

Latin America and the United States: Geographic Fatalism

Latin America experienced one of the most internationalist processes of independence which was evident from Francisco de Miranda's and Simon Bolivar's active efforts to marshal resources for their cause in England and other European countries, the broad linking of their efforts with that of the Haitian patriots and the designing of a project of Latin American integration finding its concrete expression in the political project of Greater Colombia. But at another level, Latin America was assigned the role of natural resource supplier to the industrialising powers of the West. That economic marginalisation reflected the failure of national integration efforts in the early 19th century. Latin American societies remained underdeveloped from their independence to the first decades of the 20th century because "they became dualistic societies in which the optimisation of the elite's aims was not compatible with the basic interests of the mass thus preventing the social integration of the concerned countries and establishing in them a social regime (that is, a combined regime of values, participation, power and poverty) that was not amenable to their national development".[1]

In the post-War period, the international dependence of Latin America continued, although that dependence became far more sophisticated and pervasive than during the 19th and early 20th centuries. Fernando Henrique Cardoso, one of the leading *dependencia* writers and presently President of Brazil, called it an "associated dependent development model" where "the interests of the foreign corporations became compatible with the internal prosperity of the dependent countries..."[2] The internal colonisation of Latin America by international capital and US-based multinational corporations and the unholy alliance between the national bourgeoisie, traditional elites and international actors created a "special relationship" between Latin America and the United States. That relationship was exploitative, self-serving, intimately tied to US military/security interests and resulted in the peripherisation of Latin America in the international system. It is through a critical analysis of Latin America's ties with the US that the region's position in the Third World can be fully understood.

I. Inter-American System

The economic and political history of Latin America's ties with the United States can be likened to Gabriel Garcia Marquez's novel, *One Hundred Years of Solitude*. In the novel events follow irregular and magical cycles of sorrow and frustration. US-Latin American ties too have followed Marquez's baleful cycle. Neither Franklin Roosevelt's "Good Neighbour Policy" nor John F Kennedy's "Alliance for Progress", nor Bill Clinton's promise to construct "a genuine hemispheric community of democracies" has broken this melancholy sequence.

"Gringo interests" have dominated US ties with Latin America from the days of banana republics and gunboat diplomacy to the conflicts of the Cold War. The first substantial statement of US policy towards Latin America came through the American Congress adopting the "No-Transfer Resolution" in 1811. What began as an effort to keep the British out of Florida soon expanded when, in the early 1820s, the Holy Alliance authorised France to assist Spain in recovering its American colonies. This led to the proclamation of the Monroe Doctrine, the cognitive bedrock of US policy towards Latin America. Washington's policy towards the region has been "rarely focused upon Latin Americans per se, but more upon what extra- hemispheric rivals might do in Latin America that would affect the security of the United States".[3]

During the Cold War Washington tended to consider Latin America as its natural sphere of influence working directly and indirectly to overthrow regimes close to Moscow and unabashedly supporting rightwing military dictatorship. This attitude coupled with the US interventionist role is at the root of lingering anti-Americanism in Latin America. In the 1940s and 1950s, Latin America lived through the involution of what is known as a "parish-pump policy", dominated mainly by civilian and military strongmen who gave little opportunity for ephemeral democratic experiments and kept international relations at the minimum. In most cases foreign policy was used as an instrument for pairing good relations with the adversaries of the regimes in power. Since the beginning of the 20th century the only continuing thread in Latin America's conduct of international affairs was to give preference to bilateral relations with the United States, normally on the basis of lending support to the preoccupations and projects of the State Department. As an analyst aptly put it, Latin America could develop foreign policy as it wished but only insofar as it did not threaten US interests.[4]

For a considerable number of years, Latin American countries were like a bank, a rich one, being robbed by their own people. The robbers paid no taxes and shipped their money abroad. And when the robbed, the poor and the marginalised resisted rape and pillage, military dictators and *caudillos* were installed to put them down and shut them up. Such was the hold of the military in the region that it was said Latin America had only two parties: military and the civilian. As Carlos Fuentes, celebrated Mexican writer, says, the armed forces are "the oldest and most deeply rooted Latin American institution, along with the Roman Catholic Church. Both arrived in the New World as an outgrowth of the prolonged wars of reconquest of the Muslim Spain. The Spanish crown harnessed and projected onto the conquest of America the huge dynamism of the militant Army and the militant church".[5]

With the exception of the German-modelled Chilean Army, Latin Americans have not been good militarists, as is obvious from the defeat of the Mexican General Santa Anna at the hands of the Winfield Scott to the defeat of the Argentine generals by Margaret Thatcher. However, in order to justify their existence and their huge budgets, the armies of Latin America have staged comic-opera wars against their neighbours, or have identified themselves with nationalist causes; but mostly they have turned their power against their own people. The armies have been defeated only by revolutions in Mexico (1910), Cuba (1959) and Nicaragua (1979). The military rulers often sought to create a myth that only through an end to "politics" (politics of anti-politics) could any development mission be accomplished.

Since the proclamation of the Monroe Doctrine in 1823 Latin America's interactions with the world were overwhelmingly influenced by the foreign policy goals and actions of the United States. For one thing, the military leaders and the *Caudillos* at the helm were only too keen to play second fiddle to Washington's preoccupations in the region. For another, both as individual States or groups, the countries of northern South America, the Andes, Central America and the Southern Cone had trade dealings far more with US and Europe than with each other. The United States too had declared its intentions. The much-maligned 'Monroe Doctrine' of 1823, which was intended to keep outside powers out of the region and to enhance US hegemony, was already a well tested instrument to bring Latin American countries to their knees. The US had wrested major part of territory from Mexico in the 19th century.

To Cuba, Haiti, Dominican Republic and Puerto Rico, anti-colonialism meant anti-Americanism. Few countries have been subjected to the whims and dictates of an external power as Cuba was for most of its history. To begin with, Cuba came late to independence in 1898, some 70 years after the other Latin American countries had broken loose from Spain. Moreover, Cuba's independence, culminating a 30-year history of insurrection and guerrilla warfare against the Spanish authorities, did not bring with it any real measure of national sovereignty. On the contrary, although nominally free, the Cubans in 1898 basically exchanged one imperium for another. Three months before the war against Spain ended, US troops entered the conflict. When the smoke cleared, they remained to govern the island-nation for the next four years. The withdrawal of the US Army in 1902 was a temporary retreat. US troops returned to govern Cuba from 1906 to 1909. Later, squadrons of the US marines were landed in 1912 and 1916 to help settle internal Cuban political affairs. In later years, political intervention became less direct but it was nonetheless potent. Some 60 years after Cuban independence, a former US Ambassador to Cuba could testify before the US Congress that "the United States, until the advent of Castro, was so overwhelmingly influential in Cuba that...the American Ambassador was the second most important man in Cuba; sometimes even more important than the President".[6]

The story of other Latin American countries was only partly different. Political hegemony was matched by economic influence and intervention. Thus in the 1950s and 1960s, when the US assumed a moral role of combating communism, Latin American nations had no choice but to get drawn into the Cold War as allies of the US in hemispheric solidarity against an extra-continental threat from the Soviet Union. From this evolved an inter-American system with the US as the dominant actor. It is interesting to note that at a time when the 1947 Asian Conference was organised by Nehru in New Delhi, which initiated the process of Third World solidarity, Latin American countries formally signed a mutual defence agreement with the US, called the Inter-American Treaty of Reciprocal Assistance or the Rio Pact.

Some of the objectives of the Rio Pact included "protecting the sources of strategic material and the lines of access to them; maintaining a capacity to defend the region against small aircraft and submarine attacks from the outside; and reducing the role of the US armed forces in regional defence".[7] Mario Ojeda described the 1947 treaty as the "first treaty of the Cold War"[8] which served US hemispheric and global interests. Besides securing hemispheric co-operation a network of inter-American military schools, training programmes and defence councils were developed which further tightened US grip on the region.

Way back in 1890 the United States and 18 Latin American countries formed the International Union of American Republics. The central office of this organisation, called the Commercial Bureau of the American Republics was renamed the Pan American Union in 1910. The objective of the Pan American Union was to establish closer economic, cultural and political co-operation among member countries. In reality it became an instrument for bullying the Latin American States into accepting US hegemony. The Pan American Union was the forerunner of the Organisation of American States (OAS) created in 1948, only a year after the Rio Pact was signed. The Pan-American Union convened a conference in 1945, which proclaimed the Act of Chapultepec, which was a treaty of mutual assistance. As Demetrio Boersner maintains, while Latin American countries favoured the Rio Pact of 1947 to uphold the spirit of the Act of Chapultepec which was non-interventionist in intent, the United States used the Pact to suit its anti-Communist strategic interests. "What NATO did to unite the US and Western Europe against the Soviet Union, the Inter-American Treaty of Reciprocal Assistance did by serving Washington's interests in the Western Hemisphere".[9]

During the discussion of the projected treaty, the United States wanted the Rio Pact to be invoked not just in case of direct attack against a member country but also against the "base" of a country even outside the Western Hemisphere. The Latin Americans rejected it outright. It was finally agreed that a direct attack alone would invoke the mechanisms of joint action against an aggressor. In case of an attack against an extra-continental base, the member countries would only hold consultations. Guatemala, Uruguay and Venezuela proposed that Rio Treaty be invoked in case of human rights violations in member States. But since that clause could have been used as an instrument of intervention, Mexico and certain other democratic regimes opposed it and so did the military regimes for their own selfish reasons.[10]

The Organisation of American States itself resulted from the desire to give permanent legal form to the hitherto loosely organised Pan-American Union. The OAS was formed to "promote the peaceful settlement of international disputes and to encourage.... international trade". It symbolised hemispheric co-operation under the notion that "the hemispheric States shared a common history, philosophy, and destiny that distinguished them from the rest of the world"[11] But "its headquarters in Washington remained a symbol of American dominance".[12] While both the Rio Treaty and the OAS firmly attached Latin America to the US pole, the way the inter-American system evolved over the years helped preserve the "paradigm of strategic denial" to Washington's rivals.[13]

II. Pilot-Fish Behaviour

In the 1950s, virtually every Latin American country was brought under the US military assistance programme. Latin America's arms purchase came almost entirely from the US. In 1959, the Inter-American Development Bank (IDB) was established to provide financial assistance to Latin American nations from the US and other sources. Bilateral economic assistance programme was another tool of US foreign policy in Latin America. Military intervention became the ultimate state-to-state policy instrument within Washington's Central American and Caribbean "sphere of influence". Nicaragua, Guatemala, Haiti, Mexico, Cuba and the Dominican Republic all lived through US aggression. John Foster Dulles, US Secretary of State, espoused the anti-Communist US policy. He said, "The master plan of international communism is to gain a solid base in this hemisphere, a base that can be used to extend communist penetration".[14]

The ouster of the nationalist Jacobo Arbenz Government in Guatemala in a CIA-engineered coup in 1954 was the first major test of the new US doctrine in the region, termed by one Latin American President as an "international licence to the United States to do....everything (it) pleases".[15] The Arbenz Government had only attempted to swing toward radicalism, with the backing of the Communist Party, a small but influential one that was in control of the labour movement. The Soviet

Union was accused by Washington of providing political, economic and armed support though there was little evidence pointing to direct Soviet involvement. The United States treated Guatemala as a major issue. With covert support from the CIA, anti-Arbenz forces launched an invasion from Honduras and soon overthrew the regime.[16]

Containing Communist intrusion became the overriding US goal, especially after 1959 when Cuba and Cuban Revolution became the seminal issue for US policy in Latin America. The militarist interventionist politics of the pre-"Good Neighbour" era returned, although with new ideological wrappings, in specific US policy applications. These included military intervention in Cuba (1961), intervention in Guyana via the CIA, to stop Cheddi Jagan from capturing power (1962) and the forceful frustration of a potential revolution in the Dominican Republic (1965).

The Cuban Revolution of 1959 changed the orientation of US policy towards Latin America and the inter-American system itself assumed new dimensions. From the US perspective, the concept of hemispheric defence shifted from external to internal security in which the main effort was devoted to countering internal subversions. Military aid, technical assistance became new buzzwords. In the 1960s, among the more visible results of a new change were escalated US training of Latin America's military, especially in the techniques of anti-guerrilla warfare. The overthrow of the Frondizi Government in Argentina in 1962, the ouster of the progressive Goulart Government in Brazil in 1964, the invasion of the Dominican Republic in 1965 and, as Richard Nixon himself admitted, the so-called "destabilisation" of the Salvador Allende Government in Chile in 1973 were the inevitable results of a new transformation in US-Latin American ties.

In the face of such internationalist policy, Latin American regimes displayed what may be called pilot-fish behaviour—staying close to the shark to avoid being eaten. In the 50s and early 60s most Latin American regimes followed the US lead as was evident from their voting behaviour in the UN. Jeanne Hey has described such foreign policy behaviour of Latin America as "pro-core policy" which does not "treat core powers as the inherent enemy of Latin America and…seeks to work with the core-actors to achieve foreign policy goals".[17]

The US policy concentrated upon the containment of the Cuban Revolution, pressing for the island-nation's ouster from hemispheric political and economic systems and training Latin American military to prevent its repetition elsewhere. This priority of "no more Cubas" was to shape the Latin American policy of the US for a decade – from Kennedy's 'Alliance for Progress' to Kissinger's New Dialogue. President Lyndon Johnson justified his massive Dominican intervention in 1965: "We do not propose to sit here in our rocking chair with our hands folded and let the communists set up any government in the Western Hemisphere".[18] The Bay of Pigs invasion of 1961 and the 1962 Missile Crisis, the latter being the most menacing event of the Cold War, sought to project Cuba as a threat to hemispheric security. Most Latin American regimes except Mexico, supported the US move to expel Cuba from the OAS. The "Alliance for Progress", launched in August 1961, provided the conceptual umbrella for preventing the repeat of Cuba in the region.

That the Latin American countries toed the US line was evident from the establishment of an inter-American military force during the Missile Crisis, the first time the Rio Pact was invoked to repel an action by the Soviet Union. The organ of consultation recommended to allied members that they "take all measures, individually and collectively, including the use of armed force". A combined quarantine force was established under a US commander that included two Argentine destroyers and, more "symbolically", a Dominican gunboat.

The second instance occurred in 1965, when the OAS authorised the establishment of a temporary Inter-American Peacekeeping Force. The US had landed troops in the Dominican Republic, and the force was an effort to transform that unilateral decision into a collective endeavour. At its peak, the force contained only about 2000 Latin American troops, mostly Brazilians. Costa Rica, El Salvador, Honduras, Nicaragua and Paraguay also participated in the force.

The formulation of the "Alliance for Progress" was paralleled by an increase in the penetration of the multinational corporations in Latin America. Though economic development of Latin America was the ostensible aim of the "Alliance for Progress", it led to an economic subjugation of the region. The increasing penetration of the MNCs into the internal affairs of Latin American nations had been facilitated by Latin American foreign policies seeking to enhance levels of economic development through direct investment by foreign companies. The MNCs exercised a major influence on domestic and foreign policy of Latin American countries, especially that of Peru, Bolivia, Chile and Venezuela.

As is clear from the above discussion, the United States manipulated nearly total support from Latin America for its crusade against communism. Some of the countries shared the burden of an unconventional kind. For example the United States and Honduras assisted the forces that overthrew President Arbenz of Guatemala in 1954. The US, Guatemala and Nicaragua trained and supported the Cuban exile brigade to launch the Bay of Pigs invasion in 1961. Latin America was more than willing to supply intelligence to US agencies.

III. 'New' Latin American Foreign Policy

Changes in the international system in the 1970s coupled with the US policy of "benign neglect" under the Nixon-Ford administrations and new shifts in the domestic policies of many Latin American nations led to the emergence of what one analyst calls "new" Latin American foreign policy.[19] Though the United States continued to be an important factor, Latin American foreign policy was moulded increasingly by changes external to the region such as the decline in global-level bipolarity, the emergence of détente, the rise of multi-polarity and the lessening of Washington's concern with and involvement in Latin America.

Latin America's foreign policies in the 1970s can be understood in the context of regional and global interdependence. Latin America attempted and succeeded to some extent in what one analyst called "a diversification of dependence" on the US.[20] The period saw great expansion in Latin America's international contacts. Such a goal was accomplished by securing export markets in a number of countires, acquiring imports from various supplier countires, and attracting development assistance from various contries, development financing agencies and private investors in as large a number of countries as possible instead of looking mainly to the US. Other means of diversification included the increasingly frequent practice of multilateral action, often in solidarity with other Third World nations, to make demands felt, to exert leverage, and to extract concessions. Some countries even imposed various restrictions and control on foreign investments in order to gain a greater degree of domestic economic control.

More and more countries opened diplomatic missions in other Third World countries and expanded contacts with the European Community, Canada and Japan. Significant variations were seen among Latin American countries in their bid to acquire greater leverage in international affairs. From a global perspective, "all of the Latin American countries are lesser ranking ones in terms of power and capability to act in the international system".[21] And yet, countries like Brazil, Mexico, Argentina and Venezuela, with their large internal markets, attractive investment opportunities and in some cases, the new found wealth, succeeded in diversifying their contacts. Brazil did not pursue an aggressive foreign policy nor did it pretend to lead the Third World, but it did succeed in promoting its national economic objectives. The undoctrinaire policy of pragmatic initiative resulted in Brazil forging economic ties with racist South Africa. Brazil soon replaced Portugal in terms of its extensive trade links with Africa.[22]

IV. Third Worldism under Perez, Echeverria and Velasco

In the 1970s the bargaining position of some of the Latin American countries increased considerably due primarily to their growing economic clout and the cause certain regimes sought to promote. Venezuela under Carlos Andres Perez, Mexico under Luis Echeverria and Peru under Juan Velasco Alvarado are illustrating cases in point. After the downfall of the Marcos Perez Jimenez dictatorship in 1958 the patron-client relationship between Venezuela and the US gave way to an independent line in foreign policy. Both the Social Democrat (1959-79) and the Christian Democrat (1969-1974) regimes displayed an active trajectory in the international field. However, Venezuela's position of leadership was strengthened since 1974 (a year in which the country saw its income from petroleum sales quadruple, going from 2.5 billion to 10 billion dollars) with the ever increasing opportunity to support the needs of other countries in the region.

In the early 60s, the "Betancourt Doctrine" was propounded by President Romulo Betancourt whereby Venezuela's diplomatic ties with other countries became conditioned by the principles and mechanisms of representative democracy practised in those countries. Under the Betancourt regime, Venezuela broke off diplomatic ties with Argentina, Ecuador, El Salvador, the Dominican Republic, Honduras, Peru, Nicaragua and Paraguay. Venezuela's ties with Cuba were the worst affected. The Castro regime openly financed and supported the guerrilla groups in Venezuela. Venezuela worked actively for sanctions being imposed against Cuba as also its expulsion from the OAS. The "Betancourt Doctrine" was abandoned by the Rafael Caldera administration, which followed a policy of "ideological pluralism" and resumed ties with all Latin American countries except Cuba.

The advent of the Carlos Andres Perez Government in 1974 marked a new phase in Venezuelan foreign policy. Perez entered office when Venezuela "enjoyed the economic wherewithal to support his temperamental proclivity towards a greater assumption of international responsibility".[23] Mexico too had begun to enjoy the fruits of its oil wealth. Thanks to their huge reserves of petroleum, Venezuela and Mexico saw the possibilities of leading the Third World. Suddenly they were able to play a considerably greater role in world affairs. Venezuela and Mexico are a good example of Latin American countries, which began to exercise more influence in the Third World precisely at a time they seemed no longer to belong to it.

While Perez as Betancourt's Minister of Interior had once been a fierce critic of Fidel Castro, he took the initiative in 1974 to restore diplomatic relations with Havana. In keeping with his hemispheric ambitions, Perez led the drive for the reincorporation of Cuba into the American family of nations.[24]

As we have noted earlier, Perez became a key figure in the North-South dialogue. Besides being instrumental in the formation of the Latin American Economic System, which included Cuba but excluded the US, Venezuela was the key founder of the Organisation of Petroleum Exporting Countries (OPEC). Venezuelan foreign policy goals under Perez were reflected in an Open Letter to US President Gerald Ford by Perez on September 14, 1974: "Venezuela perforce takes a sympathetic view of any attempt at finding solutions to the great problems of our time in global terms, but only if a global perspective does not mean that the large countries will prevail over the small countries. It would be dangerous, ineffective and harmful for global and universal solutions to lose sight of the fact that the world included us as well".[25] In organising the OPEC, in creating SELA, and in representing the oil-producing nations at the 1975 Paris talks on the new international economic order, Venezuela was apparently seeking both status and influence in the international system, particularly Third World affairs.

The case of Mexico is even more interesting. Mexico experienced one of the first social revolutions in the 20th century; the Mexican Revolution of 1910 preceded even the Bolshevik Revolution, institutionalised a uniquely stable political system, diminished the predatory role of the military in domestic politics and separated the State from the Church. However, Mexico traditionally followed a somewhat passive foreign policy. Except for the Lazaro Cardenas and Lopez Mateos administrations, Mexico kept its distance from foreign entanglements, declaring its principled defence of national integrity, independence, sovereignty, nationalism, equality and non-intervention.[26] The 1970s, however, saw a paradigm shift. During the Luis Echeverria Alvarez regime (1970-76), Mexico began to play an assertive role in world affairs and Echeverria was recognised as an effective and persistent spokesman of the Third World.

Luis Maira has put forward an interesting hypothesis in respect of Mexico's international policy. He says "at the times when Mexico's bargaining power (vis-à-vis the US) is increasing, it tends to guarantee its preferential link with the United States, and one notices a 'low profile' policy in its relations with the Latin American nations and with the developing world. On the contrary, in the critical stages, and at the same time as increasing tensions and eventual disagreements in its relations with Washington, the multilaterality of the international commitment and the strengthening of ties with the 'Third World' are favoured".[27]

Olga Pellicer too has expounded a similar thesis. As she says, "Mexican leaders' support for the so-called revolutionary regimes has had the intended objective of using it as an element of internal stability as also an instrument to strengthen the government's position vis-à-vis diverse social sectors".[28] Echeverria as Home Minister under President Diaz Ordaz was blamed for the massacre at Tlatelolco in 1968. His alignment with leftist causes at the international level was intended to have domestic pay off. As de Brody says, "it was essentially thanks to foreign policy postures that the government was able to move closer to intellectuals like Octavio Paz and Carlos Fuentes who wield so much influence on public opinion".[29]

Foreign policy under the Echeverria Administration was in essence and in substance a departure from the past because it abandoned the purely defensive and isolationist strategies of its predecessors in favour of a more active and involved relationship with the world. What started as a relatively unpoliticised" commercial diplomacy" of his first few years in office became a "highly politicised activism".[30] As the years passed by, Echeverria had evolved a leftist, activist foreign policy devoted to global change.[31] Besides solidarity with Cuba, the Mexican government openly came out in support of the Salvador Allende regime in Chile. Echeverria chose forums and created platforms where the United States was not predominant or where big power interests were only equally weighted.

Mexico took a leading role in seeking a reorganisation of the international system to better represent the interests of the Third World. Echeverria's Charter of Economic Rights and Duties of States, which became a principal working document for the Third World, was endorsed by the UN General Assembly over the opposition of the US. The Charter was overwhelmingly endorsed by the vast majority of the UN's Third World members. The Charter which 'diagnosed the ills of the old order" and suggested "resolutions and codes of conduct in relations between the North and the South", turned out to be a 'declaration of redistributive justice which bestowed a patina of prestige to Mexican foreign policy".[32] Echeverria's 1974 tour of the Third World was a vigorous demonstration of Mexico's claim to the Third World leadership. Echeverria acquired an image of a "Third World reform monger" for he remained active in the politics of the developing world while ignoring membership in the UN Security Council and avoiding the OAS, both of which represented big power interests. In order to compensate for the pronouncedly anti-US foreign policy stances, Echeverria left doors open to US investments, particularly in sectors not reserved for the State.

Mexico's foreign policy under Lopez Portillo too remained oriented towards the Third World, though the rhetoric of the Echeverria period gave way to pragmatism. The discovery of oil increased its leverage vis-à-vis the US and gave it manoeuvring room within which some defiance of the northern neighbour was possible and tolerated. Mexico's activist policy in Central America was the result of the country's increased prosperity. In the later years of the Portillo's presidency, Mexico sought a leadership role in the Central American region. In 1980 Portillo undertook a six-nation tour of Latin American countries. Behind this lay Portillo's desire to form a united front against a possible return of Cold War politics to the region. Portillo's tour covered all shades of the political spectrum, from Cuba to Brazil, by way of Nicaragua, Panama, Venezuela and Costa Rica. The trip culminated in the formal signing of the agreement by which Mexico and Venezuela undertook to fulfil all the imported oil requirements of nine Central American and Caribbean countries on favourable terms.

By far the most provocative part of the tour, as far as the US is concerned, was the highly successful 3-day trip to Cuba. The final communiqué included most of the Non-Aligned Movement's favourite themes, from opposition to all "hegemonies' and the nefarious activities of the MNCs, to support for the right of all peoples to choose their own form of government. The communiqué also denounced the US blockade of Cuba. Portillo's tour was acclaimed as a triumph for Mexico's drive to establish itself as an important actor on the world stage. Though Portillo had no intention to deliberately provoke the US, his defiance on such issues as Iran, the Olympic Games in Moscow, tuna fishing and Cuba was designed to consolidate Mexico's position as a leader of the Third World. Just as Echeverria stopped short of becoming officially a member of NAM or OPEC, the Lopez Portillo regime eventually rejected membership in the General Agreement on Trade and Tariffs (GATT).

In 1968, the Peruvian armed forces overthrew the civilian government of President Belaunde Terry and took significant political steps within an authoritarian framework, which caught the imagination of many Third World nations. The Juan Velasco Alvarado regime dramatically reoriented Peruvian foreign policy and took positions in defiance of the US. Velasco took the lead in demanding a radical reorganisation of the inter-American system. It sought closer association with the NAM countries and actively supported the demand for the establishment of a New International Economic Order.

V. Latin Leaders Speak Gringo

The 1980s and 1990s have seen a sea change in Latin America's ties with the US. While democratic regimes have totally replaced the military dictatorships, the harsh anti-American posturing is fast dissolving. Today, the US and Latin America speak the same economic language-that of free trade between free markets. There has been a change of another kind as well. The Latin American leaders today include alumni of Yale, Columbia and the University of Michigan. And they see the United States not so much as the overbearing behemoth of Latin lore, but as a place where they studied, whose language they share and whose values they are fast embracing.

Indeed, the ornate Spanish-style presidential palaces of Latin America are increasingly filled with leaders who mowed lawns during summer jobs in the US. Mexican President Ernesto Zedillo earned a doctorate in economics from Yale. President Alberto Fujimori of Peru studied at the University of Michigan. President Fernando Henrique Cardoso of Brazil lectured at Stanford and Princeton. Former Bolivian President Gonzalo Sanchez grew up in the US and speaks Spanish with an American accent. This prompted an analyst to say, "the best US investment in Latin America was not the Alliance for Progress, but the Fulbright scholars programme".[33]

For decades, Latin America looked on the United States as a big, oppressive power determined to exploit its smaller, weaker neighbours to the South. Most Latin American governments defined their foreign policy primarily in opposition to the United States either by denouncing US imperialism and interventionism or bemoaning their dependence on the "Colossus of the North". In the process, if ideological spats hindered a meaningful dialogue, the lack of communication only bred further resentment. All this has changed. Today there is greater convergence in the Americas, North and South on political values and economic fundamentals than ever before. The motto of the 60s, 'Yankee go home', has been replaced by 'Yankee, please come' in the 90s.

All the Latin American countries have made a 180-degree shift in their policy stances—from a confrontational policy to a conciliatory policy towards the United States by not only liberalising the economy but also removing all possible obstacles to a closer relationship with Washington. The scenario in the 1990s is somewhat similar to the 1930s when the US and Latin America moved closer in terms of bilateral trade relations. If Latin America has been unable to make a dent in Europe, the United States has found it equally hard to penetrate Japan. About 50 per cent of Latin American export today are destined for the American markets. The US, on its part, is now exporting more to Latin America than to Japan, and Germany. The rate of increase in US exports to Latin

America for the past three years has been three times as great as that for all other regions.

Shortly after assuming office, the Bush administration unveiled the "Brady Plan" for reducing Latin America's commercial bank debt. The plan endorsed extensive debt relief for Latin America's heavily indebted countries. Two weeks after Washington's decision to pursue free-trade talks with Mexico, President Bush launched his 'Enterprise for the Americas Initiative' in June 1990 which envisioned a free-trade zone from Alaska to Tierra del Fuego. Latin American leaders began to compete for Bush's attention ever since. Three days after the announcement, the Chilean Economy Minister Alexandro Foxley was knocking on the White House door, explaining why Chile deserved a free-trade agreement as much as Mexico.

In December 1990, Bush undertook a visit to Brazil, Uruguay, Argentina, Chile and Venezuela. Unlike Reagan, who marvelled after his one trip to South America that the countries there were really different from one another, Bush's visit was a successful one. His visit was the first by a US chief executive to Brazil since 1982, to Uruguay since 1967, to Venezuela since 1978 and to Chile and Argentina since 1960. The Enterprise for the Americas Initiative was the result of the realisation that in the post-Cold War era, hemispheric partnerships would be helpful to the US. It promised a reduction of Latin America's official debt owed to US government agencies, offered aid to facilitate investment in the region and held out the prospect of free-trade agreements. Besides an emerging consensus between US and Latin America on economic reforms, US-Latin American ties also acquired some warmth as far as their renewed interest in the Organisation of American States is concerned. For long the United States ignored the OAS in times of crisis situations, pursued its own agenda. However, the OAS, which often got paralysed in the past, has been activated once again. This has been possible because of Latin America's democratisation and a growing convergence between the US and Latin America on regional issues.

The end of the Cold War marked a new phase in Latin America's ties with the US during the Clinton administration. Clinton has made economics, especially economic integration through market opening as the main focus of his Latin American policy. Whereas his Cold War predecessors spent much of their time re-engineering governments throughout Latin America to suit the interests of the US foreign policy, Clinton has emphasised the mutual economic benefits to be gained from the trade.

The signing of the North American Free Trade Agreement (NAFTA) in 1993, with its inclusion of Mexico, held out the promise that open markets would produce opportunities for the rest of the Americas, not just for the rich northern powers.[34] At the Miami Summit of the Americas in December 1994, Clinton and 33 other Western Hemisphere heads of State established the goal of concluding arrangements for Free Trade Areas of Americas (FTAA) by 2005. It was an ambitious goal, which has become the cornerstone of US-Latin American ties. The Miami moment was the high-water mark of US engagement with Latin America. It was followed almost immediately by the Mexican Peso crisis, which raised anti-free trade opinion in the US. Clinton's failure to secure legislation for "fast track" trade negotiating authority has been viewed in Latin America as a big letdown.

The United States has profited substantially from Latin American economic reform and the new 'partnership" with the region. Latin America has become more vital to the United States. US exports to the region grew 24.3 per cent in 1997, making it the fastest-growing market for American goods in the world. According to the US Commerce Department projections, Latin America will overtake Europe and Asia to become the biggest US trading partner within the next decade. The US trade with Mexico touched a $160 billion figure in 1997, which rivals US-Japan commerce, thanks in part to NAFTA. US companies sold more to Brazil in 1996 than to China. Even Central America today buys more US goods than Eastern Europe and the former Soviet Union combined.

Clinton has made three trips to Latin America, the last being in October 1997. Overall these visits have not produced the kind of dramatic moments or historic treaties that have marked the American

President's visit to Europe and the former Soviet Union. The next few years could see growing diplomatic tensions between the US and its southern neighbours who fear Washington is about to close the door on their hopes of getting unfettered access to US markets.

The fantastic statistics on Latin America's economic growth and trade expansion have hardly improved life for the majority of the region's citizens. Income gap between rich and poor has only widened further. As Jorge Castaneda says, "trade liberalisation has helped control inflation and increase productivity, technology transfer and exports. But on the other hand the flood of imports from the United States has destroyed millions of jobs in traditional industry and agriculture".[35] If the employment and real wage situation does not improve, "the hypothetical benefits of free trade will be ephemeral, modest and possibly even counter-productive in the long term".[36]

With the ultimate fate of the "fast track" hanging in balance, Latin America already looks like a spurned lover. Washington has been flirting for sometime now but it can't decide if it really wants a serious relationship. The whole mood of convergence among the Americas is beginning to dissipate. The sense in Latin America that the FTAA had become the latest in a series of failed post-Second World War political initiatives towards Latin America would be combined with doubt about Washington's approach to the region in the years to come. As one analyst maintains," if trade was the carrot for Latin America in its relations with the US, now all that remain was the stick, on issues such as drugs and immigration." The US has a long history of raising Latin America's expectations only to dash them. Latin America may have its own reasons to accept a North American embrace. One only hopes it doesn't end in tears.

Notes and References

1.   Helio Jaguaribe, *Political Development: A General Theory and a Latin American Case Study* (New York: Harper & Row, 1973), p. 431.

2. Fernando Henrique Cardoso, "Associated–Dependent Development: Theoretical and Practical Implications", in Alfred Stepan, (ed.), *Authoritarian Brazil* (New Haven, Conn: Yale University Press, 1973), p. 149.

3. Lars Schoultz, "US-Latin American Relations", in Joel Krieger,(ed.) *The Oxford Companion to Politics of the World* (New York: Oxford University Press, 1993), p. 947.

4. Gerhard Drekonja-Kornat, "The Rise of Latin America's Foreign Policy between Hegemony and Autonomy", *Latin American Research Review,* Vol. 21, No. 1, 1986, p. 241.

5. Carlos Fuentes, "Power against the People", *Newsweek,* April 21, 1986, p. 39.

6. Testimony of Earl Smith, Ambassador to Cuba from 1957 to January 1959, before the US Congress.

7. For the detailed analysis of the Rio Pact, see Edwin Lieuwen, *Survey of the Alliance for Progress* (Washington DC: US Senate Committee on Foreign Relations, 1967), pp. 21-22.

8. Mario Ojeda Gomez, "The United States-Latin American Relationship since 1960", *The World Today*, Vol. 30, December 1974, p. 514.

9. Demetrio Boersner, *Relaciones Internacionales de America Latina* (Caracas: Editorial Nueva Sociedad, 1990), p. 237.

10. *Ibid.*

11. Jerome Slater, *The OAS and United States Foreign Policy* (Columbus: Ohio State University Press, 1967). Also see, Ann Van Wynen Thomas and A J Thomas, *The Organisation of the American States* (Dallas: Southern Methodist University Press, 1963) and M.Margaret Ball, *The OAS Transition* (Durhan, North Carolina: Duke University Press, 1969).

12. Gerald Segal, *The World Affairs Companion* (London: Simon & Schuster, 1993), p. 240.

13. Lars Schoultz, *Op. Cit.*, p. 948.

14. Dulles quoted in Ydigoras Fuentes, *My War with Communism* (Englewood Cliffs, N J: Prentice-Hall, Inc; 1963), pp. 50-51.

15. Richard Millett, "Imperialism, Intervention, and Exploitation: The Historical Context of International Relations in the Caribbean", in Richard Millett and W Marvin Will (eds.), *The Restless Caribbean: Changing Patterns of International Relations* (New York: Praeger Publishers, 1979), pp. 14-18.

16. For detailed analysis of US game in Central America and elsewhere in Latin America, see Cole Blasier, *The Hovering Giant: US Responses to Revolutionary Change in Latin America* (Pittsburgh: Pittsburgh University Press, 1976).

17. Jeanne A K Hey, "Three Building Blocks of a Theory of Latin American Foreign Policy", *Third World Quarterly,* Vol. 18, No. 4, 1997, p. 663.

18. Johnson quoted in Martin J Sherwin and Peter Winn, "The US and Cuba", *The Wilson Quarterly* ,Winter 1978, p. 67.

19. Gerhard Drekonja-Kornat, quoted in Jeanne A K Hey, *Op. Cit.*, p. 634.

20. James D Cochrane, "Characteristics of Contemporary Latin American International Relations", *Journal of Inter-American Studies and World Affairs*, Vol. 20,No. 4, November 1978, p. 457.

21. *Ibid*, p. 458.

22. For detailed analysis of Brazilian foreign policy, see, Wolf Grabendorff, "La Politica Exterior del Brazil: Entre el Primer y Tercer Mundo", *Nueva Sociedad* (San Jose), No 41, March-April 1979, pp. 108-120; Riordan Roett, "Brazil Ascendant: International Relations and Geopolitics in the Late 20th Century", *Journal of International Affairs*, Vol. 29, No. 2, Fall 1975, pp. 139-154; and Norman A Bailey and Ronald M Schneider, "Brazil's Foreign Policy: A Case Study in Upward Mobility", *Inter-American Economic Affairs*, Vol. 27, No. 4, Spring 1974, pp. 3-25.

23. John D Martz, "Ideology and Oil: Venezuela in the Circum-Caribbean", in H Michael Erisman and John D Martz, (eds.) *Colossus Challenged* (Boulder, Colorado: Westview Press, 1982), p. 123.

24. *Ibid*, p. 125.

25. "In Defence of our Resources", An Open Letter from President Carlos Andres Perez to President Gerald Ford, September 19, 1974, as quoted in Riordan Roett, *Latin America in the 1980s: Socio-Political Perspectives* (Washington , D.C: The Johns Hopkins University, 1976), p. 47.

26. Mario Ojeda, *Alcances y Limites de la Politica Exterior de Mexico* (El Colegio de Mexico, 1976), p. 3.

27. Luis Maira, "Caribbean State Systems and Middle-Status Powers: The Cases of Mexico, Venezuela, and Cuba", in Paget Henry and Carl Stone (eds.), *The Newer Caribbean : Decolonisation, Democracy and Development* (Philadelphia: Institute for the Study of Human Issues, 1983), p. 191.

28. Olga Pellicer de Brody, "Veinte Anos de Politica Exterior Mexicana: 1960-1980", *Foro Internacional* (Mexico City), Vol. 21, No. 2, October-December 1980, p. 151.

29. *Ibid*.

30. Guy Poitras, "Mexico's Foreign Policy in an Age of Interdependence", in Elizabeth G Ferris and Jennie K Lincoln, *Op. Cit.*, p. 107. For an elaborate discussion of Mexico's foreign policy. See, *Continuidad y Cambio en la Politica Exterior de Mexico*, 1977, Centro de Estudios Internacionales, El Colegio de Mexico, 1977.

31. William Hamilton, "Mexico's 'New' Foreign Policy: A Re-examination", *"Inter-American Economic Affairs*, Vol. 29, Winter 1975, p. 54.

32. Guy Poitras, *Op.Cit.*, p. 107.

33. *Peru Economico*, October 1994.

34. For a detailed analysis of US-Latin American ties in the 1990s, see, Peter Hakim, "NAFTA and After: A New Era for the United States and Latin America?", *Current History,* Vol. 93, No. 581, March 1994, pp. 97-102; Abraham F Lowenthal, "Latin America: Ready for Partnership?" *Foreign Affairs,* Vol 72. No1, 1993, pp. 74-92 and Peter Hakim, "Clinton and Latin America: Facing an Unfinished Agenda", *Current History,* Vol. 92, No. 572, March 1993, pp. 97-101.

35. Jorge Castaneda, "The Might-Have-Been Summit", *Newsweek*, April 27, 1998, p. 21.

36. *Ibid.*

4

Latin America and the Non-Aligned Movement: The Achilles Heel

For three and a half centuries, the sovereign nation-states had a limited choice in foreign affairs. Imperialism, Universalism, isolationism, alliances, neutrality, balance of power etc., were the hallmarks of traditional foreign policy which became "obsolescent, if not altogether obsolete" at the end of the Second World War.[1] The Second World War sounded the death-knell of imperialism, giving rise to the emergence of dozens of independent States, particularly in Asia and Africa. Other traditional foreign policy orientations too lost their relevance and appeal in the radically transformed global environment. Whether protagonists of Non-Alignment like it or not, Non-Alignment was a product of Cold War and an attendant phenomenon of the bloc division. The ethos of Non-Alignment of course preceded the Cold War, but without Cold War divisions, the Non-Aligned Movement (NAM) may not have found an institutional expression at all.

I. Defining Non-Alignment

The Non-Aligned countries represent a wide spectrum of political philosophies, economic strategies and socio-cultural backgrounds. Non-Alignment has come to mean many things to many States. As Leo Mates, who was the secretary-general of the 1961 Belgrade Summit, says, "there are at least as many possible definitions of Non-Alignment as there are Non-Aligned countries". Many newly independent States joined NAM only to protect their sovereign status from erosion through alliances with big powers, and not to create a movement for unity of action. To say that the policy of Non-Alignment was in the best interests of the newly decolonised States is to make a virtue of the necessity, for there were no other viable policy options left to them.

India saw in Non-Alignment the fulfilment of Gandhiji's hopes that freedom must be part of the struggle for emancipation of all peoples. Former President of Sri Lanka J R Jayewardene found in the movement all the traits of Asoka's teachings. While presenting his report in Havana as outgoing Chairman of NAM, President Jayewardene spoke at length about the philosophical foundations of the movement. He said: "The great Emperor Asoka of India, in the third century BC, sent his son, the Arahat Mahinda, to preach the Buddha Dhamma to the king of Sri Lanka Devanam Piyatissa and his people. Since then, for over 2300 years, the majority of our people have attempted in our humble ways to follow this teaching of peace and non-violence. Asoka's benign views were inscribed in rock edicts, one of which enjoined his people not to extol one's own sect or disparage another's:

> On each occasion we should honour
> Another man's sect, for by doing so
> One increases the influence of one's own
> Sect and benefits that of the other man

Translated into modern political terms, this instruction gives us a firm philosophical base for tolerance, mutual respect, non-aggression and co-existence—all essential features of Non-Alignment as we understand and practise it".[2]

According to Adam Malik of Indonesia, "The policy of Non-Alignment – or independent and active foreign policy, as we ourselves call it – is one to which Indonesia already committed itself from its very birth as an independent republic in 1945, long before the advent of the movement itself".[3] As a Latin American leader said, his country had its own peculiar reasons to join NAM. Aristides Royo made an interesting presentation: "Some years ago, a Latin American leader, desperate because his people had already spent many years trying to fight against the colonialist presence in a Latin American country, took a long trip and, one afternoon, met with Marshal Tito of Yugoslavia and told him about his feelings of desperation,…Marshal Tito's advice to him was: Join the Non-Aligned countries'. And that is how Panama became a member of the Movement of Non-Aligned countries, and that leader— General Omar Torrijos – now testifies with his presence here…".[4]

To Gustavo Fernandez, Minister of Foreign Affairs of Bolivia,"Non-alignment really is alignment with freedom and justice, alignment against all forms of exploitation and economic and political oppression of the Third World countries".[5] Ethiopian leader Mengistu Haile Mariam sought to give a radical interpretation of NAM. He said: "when innocent blood of the oppressed masses is being shed with impunity, 'Non-alignment' cannot and should not mean utter indifference. While a struggle is being waged against oppression, exploitation and backwardness and while a life-and-death struggle is raging on the battlefield against anti-people forces, our Movement cannot be a refuge for fence-sitters".[6]

The Non-Aligned Movement, "born of the yoke of domination, oppression and racism in mankind's irreversible march towards emancipation and liberation in the quest for well-being and happiness, in the struggle for survival, has become a living dynamic reality".[7] According to President Ahmed Sekou Toure of Guinea, "Non-Alignment does not mean non-involvement or indifference, for we are neither neutral nor indifferent in choosing between what is good and what is bad; we have chosen between colonisation and national independence; we have chosen between apartheid and racial equality; we have chosen between the economic enslavement of nations and the free and full enjoyment of the people's productive efforts".[8]

To Samora Machel, President of Mozambique, "Non-alignment means just one thing: everybody lined up together in the fight against imperialism". The ideology of NAM, according to Machel, is "based on the people's interests and the struggle against the exploitation of man by man. It is anti-fascist and is against tyrannies and dictatorships...an instrument for the political, economic, social and cultural liberation of our peoples. A consistent liberation struggle must necessarily be anti-imperialist".[9] "Socialist countries," according to Machel, "are natural allies of our peoples...we say this as a Non-Aligned country which knows and lives reality and history...".[10]

Tanzanian President Julius Nyerere, however, differed with that interpretation: "Our movement is a progressive one, but it is not a movement of progressive States. We have socialists among us, but we are not a movement of socialist States. From the very beginning we have had States that claim allegiance to socialism, and some that aspire to construct capitalism and still others that say they are neither socialists nor capitalists! We would not form another power bloc, even if we wanted to".[11] Boutros Boutros-Ghali, also echoed somewhat similar sentiment when he said "Non-Alignment cannot, itself, become a coalition, a bloc, since that would imply broadening and deepening the tyrannies of the Cold War".[12]

As we have seen, some countries openly sought to take the Non-Aligned Movement closer to the Socialist bloc, while others tried to make NAM a proxy for the Western bloc. In reality, both the Soviet Union and the Western bloc nations had denounced Non-Alignment as an immoral doctrine. Both camps contended that there could be no neutrals in the Holy crusade the Superpowers had launched. Sinnathanby Rajaratnam, Foreign Minister of Singapore held the view that the Communist bloc "supported anti-imperialism not because it loved us.... (but because it) saw in our struggle a means of weakening its Western rivals".[13] NAM leaders often resorted to plain sophistry while defining Non-alignment. According to Krishna Menon, "a non-aligned nation must be non-aligned with the non-aligned to be truly non-aligned."

II. Historic Context

The Non-Aligned Movement originated as a bi-continental initiative. Asia and Africa had little in common except profound anti-colonial sentiment and a strong sense of nationalism. As Natwar Singh maintains, Bandung, Brioni, and Belgrade are "important landmarks" in the evolution of NAM, but its beginning "goes back to the Haripura Session of the All India Congress Committee in early 1938".[14] Jawaharlal Nehru laid the philosophical foundation of India's foreign policy which also became the guiding principle of NAM. Nehru said, "Independent India would keep aloof from both imperialism and fascism". Nehru later said: "We propose, as far as possible, to keep away from the power politics of groups, aligned against one another which have led in the past to world wars and which may again lead to disasters on an even vaster scale".[15]

Before countries of Asia and Africa emerged on the world scene as a group, Asian countries held several pan-Asiatic conferences. One such conference was held in Nagasaki, Japan, in 1926 convened by Japanese parliamentarians. Japan, China, India, Afghanistan, Malaysia and Korea attended the conference. It was the first international manifestation of Asian solidarity. The conference recommended, among other things, the creation of "the League of Asian People", with its headquarters in Tokyo. Japan convened another conference in Tokyo in 1943 where delegates of countries controlled by Japan were present. Besides calling for the independence of the Philippines, Burma, Indonesia, Malaysia and Singapore, the conference demanded the elimination of Western influence and Communism in Asia. According to Uldaricio Figueroa Pla, "this attitude of equidistance and equal hostility towards colonialism and communism marked the first step towards non-alignement".[16]

In March 1947, India convened the Asian Relations Conference in New Delhi, which, many analysts believe, was the forerunner of the Non-Aligned Movement. Though it met only at the non-governmental level, it gave a call to support the liberation movements, end to foreign domination and imperialism, elimination of racial discrimination, reordering of the colonial economic system and creation of an "Asian Relations

Organisation" to promote co-operation among the peoples of the region. The Second Asian Relations Conference was convened by Nehru in January 1949. Australia and New Zealand too participated in the conference. Africa was represented by Ethiopia and Egypt. China and the Asian Republics of the Soviet Union, however, did not participate. It was here that the Afro-Asian group was formed even though it was meant primarily to promote co-operation among the would-be members of the UN.

The origin of the Non-Aligned Movement in the formal sense can be traced to the Colombo Powers Conference held in April 1954. It was here that the word "non-aligned" was first used at an international conference. The Colombo Powers held two conferences at Bogor and Bandung in Indonesia in 1954 and 1955. An offshoot of the Asian Relations Conference of 1947, Bandung signalled the first collective bid by African and Asian countries to assert their identity independent of the big powers. Colonialism, neutrality and economic development were the three main themes of the Summit deliberations attended by 29 Afro-Asian government delegations. Besides, Bandung denounced all forms of racial discrimination, particularly in South Africa, and recognised the rights of the Palestinian people.

The Bandung Conference enunciated 10 principles to guide international relations. These included:

- Respect for rights of man
- Respect for sovereignty and territorial integrity of all States
- Equality among races and nations
- Non-intervention in the internal affairs of States
- Right to legitimate individual and collective defence
- Rejection of the recourse to military alliances to defend the interest of big powers
- Abstention of the use of force
- Peaceful solution of controversies

- Favouring international co-operation

- Respect for international obligations

The concept of non-alignment played an important role in the Bandung deliberations and it is this summit conference which gave impulse to the movement transforming the essentially Afro-Asian initiative into a Non-Aligned Movement a few years later. The conference condemned "colonialism in all its manifestations". As the Indonesian diplomat, Roeslan Abdulgani, who was conference secretary general, recalls: "Turkey insists, and also Pakistan insists, and Ceylon insists that communism is a new form of colonialism. And if we say that colonialism should be abolished, then you should also fight against communism. My god, there was an uproar from China, from Vietnam".[17]

The economic development also formed an important part of the Bandung deliberations. It rejected the formation of regional blocs as a solution to the problems of international co-operation. The conference rejected the formation of political and military blocs. However, it favoured co-operation among Afro-Asian States, particularly in the field of foreign investment.

Three conferences were held in subsequent years in Brioni in July 1956, in Cairo in June 1961 and in Belgrade prior to the Summit where Bandung was elaborately discussed. By now Yugoslavia had joined the group. The texts of Brioni still referred to "Afro-Asian Non-Alignment". Gradually the term "Afro-Asian" was abandoned and the use of the term "Non-alignment" became common. The Non-Aligned Movement evolved as a unique international organisation. It had no constitution, defining its role, objectives or methodology and as M S Rajan says, it was perhaps for the same reason that Jawaharlal Nehru was not "initially enthusiastic about the holding of the first Belgrade Non-Aligned Summit in 1961".[18] Besides, when the "first Belgrade Summit conference was held, nobody, not even Tito of Yugoslavia, had thought of holding a second such conference. It was meant to be a one-time, and an ad hoc conference".[19]

Marshal Tito set forth rather eloquently the objectives of the Non-

Aligned Movement. He paid glowing tributes to the Bandung Conference and the principles enunciated there which according to him were "the first powerful display of the contemporary view of international relations" after the adoption of the UN Charter. "It was no accident", Tito said, "that these principles were proclaimed precisely in Asia, in the presence of the representatives of the peoples of Asia and Africa, the two continents inhabited by the largest number of people on our planet, who had been enslaved, deprived of rights and subject to discrimination through many centuries".[20] Tito further said, "In the same way as the Bandung Conference, and other similar conferences which followed, did not intend to establish any kind of bloc, the present conference does not pursue any such aim either. On the contrary, this conference should adopt a negative attitude towards bloc exclusiveness, which not only constitutes a threat to world peace, but also prevents other countries from participating as equal partners in the solving of outstanding international issues".[21]

Tito took pains to remove any doubts about the Non-Aligned countries forming a Third bloc. As he said, "we cannot pursue such aims as they would run counter to the political concept of non-aligned countries". Instead, the objective of the summit meeting was to tell the world that "the majority of the world decisively rejects the use of force as a means for settling the various important problems we have inherited from the last war".[22]

III. Latin America's Isolation

As we have noted earlier, Latin American countries, in the immediate aftermath of the Second World War, began the process of formally entering into an alliance with the United States. It was the time when Afro-Asian countries were engaged in laying the ideological and philosophical foundation of the Non-Aligned Movement. To wit, Latin American countries were integrated into the Inter-American Treaty of Reciprocal Assistance or the Rio Pact, which was indeed a mutual defence pact with the US. A year later, the Organisation of American States (OAS) was born. The Rio Pact was supplemented over the years by bilateral treaties whereby the United States provided military assistance to most Latin American countries.

In 1954, a year before the Afro-Asian Conference US Secretary of State John Foster Dulles used the inter-American conference held in Caracas to denounce communist actions in Latin America as "an intervention in the American affairs". In 1958, the so-called *Operacion Panamericana* was unveiled whereby Brazilian President J Kubitschek called for a reorientation of the continental policy and Latin America's vigorous participation in hemispheric affairs. President Kennedy's much hyped "Alliance for Progress" was launched in August 1961, only a month prior to the first NAM Summit in Belgrade.

Latin America's role in the Non-Aligned Movement has been much misunderstood and misinterpreted. As the discussions so far amply demonstrate, Latin America was very much part of the US sphere of influence. Besides, politically, economically and militarily, Latin America remained tied closely to the inter-American system. It therefore remained peripheral to the Non-Aligned Movement in the initial years. One also needs to understand the differences that separate Latin American countries from those of Africa and Asia. These differences include their European ethnic composition, Western cultural values and traditional trans-Atlantic trading patterns. Unlike the countries of Asia and Africa, the process of decolonisation was long over in Latin America. NAM was therefore rightly perceived in the region as an Afro-Asian movement. Given their experiences in nation-building and higher levels of economic development, Latin America had every reason to resent the leadership of the newly decolonised States.

There are many Latin American analysts who trace the origin of NAM to the concept of *justicialismo* propounded by Juan Domingo Peron of Argentina. Peron expounded a foreign policy position which came to be known as *la tercera posicion*, the third way, different from the one followed by the two superpowers.[23]

Argentina's Under-Secretary for Foreign Affairs Carlos Roberto Francisco Cavandoli traces the genesis of NAM to the inter-American system: "Belonging as we do to the Western Hemisphere, because of geographic reasons and common historical and cultural roots,...the guiding principles (of NAM) were proclaimed and enshrined in the inter-American system, which was the first organised attempt at harmonious co-existence among States within a region. Long before the creation of the League of Nations, our countries had formulated the Pan-American Union, which became, years later, the present Organisation of American States".[24] He further pointed out that "the historic and humanistic traditions of this continent" provided a great source of inspiration to the Non-Aligned Movement.

Cuba was the only country from Latin America to attend the Belgrade Summit in September 1961. It had its own compelling reasons to join the movement. Cuba, which faced near total isolation in the Western Hemisphere, needed NAM for the survival of the 1959 Revolution. But as Uldaricio Figueroa Pla maintains, Havana's stand prevented many Latin American countries from joining the Non-Aligned Movement. While in Brioni, Yugoslavia was the only country outside Asia and Africa which was present, Cuba attended the preparatory conference prior to the first NAM Summit held in Cairo in June 1961.

The Cairo meeting set out the Summit agenda and fixed five criteria for defining a non-aligned State. These included: independent policy based on political co-existence, support for the national liberation movement, non-adherence to any military alliance in the framework of super power conflicts, no bilateral alliance with super powers and non-acceptance of military bases in its territory. Twenty-one countries including Cuba participated in the preparatory committee which decided whom to invite for the Summit meeting. Argentina, Chile, Costa Rica and Paraguay figured among countries from Latin America that could be invited to the Belgrade Summit. But Cuba opposed them. "Cuba asserted its position that in the American continent political revolution must prevail over the exigency of Non-Alignment".[25]

The Belgrade Declaration's reference to Latin America was almost entirely devoted to Cuba. It said, Cuba had a right "to freely choose" its political and social system "in accordance with" its "own conditions, needs and possibilities". It further said that the North American military base at Guantanamo, Cuba, "affects the sovereignty and territorial integrity of that country".[26] The Belgrade Declaration's reference to Latin America was couched in vague generalities. For example, it said: "Imperialism is weakening, colonial empires and other forms of foreign oppression of people in Asia, Africa and Latin America are gradually disappearing from the stage of history...the peoples of Latin America are continuing to make an increasingly effective contribution to the improvement of international relations".[27]

Though no new member from Latin America joined NAM during the Cairo conference (1964), States with observer status were almost exclusively from Latin America – Argentina, Bolivia, Brazil, Chile, Jamaica, Mexico, Trinidad & Tobago, Uruguay and Venezuela. Latin American issues again did not figure prominently in the 'programme for peace and international co-operation' adopted by the Summit. It condemned "the manifestations of colonialism and neo-colonialism in Latin America" and supported "the right of peoples to self-determination and independence". The conference declaration however said all that Cuba wanted it to say like requesting the US "to lift the commercial and economic blockade applied against Cuba over the base of Guantanamo which constituted "a violation of Cuba's sovereignty and territorial integrity".[28]

Participating in the Cairo conference Cuban President Osvaldo Dorticos sought to establish a linkage between the Non-Aligned Movement and the struggle for peace and socialism",[29] an interpretation few Latin American countries were willing to subscribe to. In fact one of the reasons why Latin American countries were not enamoured of NAM was the Cuban role in it. Cuba was no role model for them. On the contrary, they were all working to avoid the creation of other Cubas in the Western Hemisphere.

When the Lusaka Summit was held in 1970, Cuba was still the lone representative from Latin America as a full-fledged member of the movement. However, three Caribbean States – Guyana, Jamaica and Trinidad and Tobago joined the group. Of the nine countries, which attended the Summit as observers, eight were from Latin America – Argentina, Barbados, Bolivia, Brazil, Chile, Colombia, Peru and Venezuela. Surprisingly the Lusaka Declaration was totally silent as far as Latin American issues were concerned.

IV. Latin-Americanisation of NAM

There were several factors why the Latin American countries remained a marginal player both in Third World politics and the Non-Aligned Movement during the 1960s. And yet, new trends such as Third Worldism in world politics slowly began to take roots in the region.

As Demitrio Boersner says, the year 1968 marked the beginning of a national surge and social change in Latin America. Latin America's international links were diversified and foreign policy acquired a complex character. Besides the Cuban Revolution, other anti-hegemonistic movements acquired a momentum. All that was happening when imperialism faced a crisis of self-confidence. While the world capitalist system was confronted with inflationary and recessionary crisis, the Vietnam War had forced the Nixon-Kissinger administration to adopt a more realistic vision towards Latin America.[30]

The 1970s marked the Latin American phase of the Non-Aligned Movement. Not only more and more Latin American and Caribbean countries joined the Movement, the region also held important NAM meetings – Ministerial conference at Georgetown (1972), Ministerial Meeting of the Co-ordinating Bureau in Havana (1975) the Co-ordination Bureau Meeting in Lima (1975) and the Sixth NAM Summit in Havana (1979). Meeting for the first time in the Latin American and the Caribbean region, the NAM Foreign Ministers attending the Georgetown conference devoted considerable time to Latin American issues. It examined the situation in Latin America and expressed full support for the Salvador Allende regime in Chile, the nationalist measures taken by the Peruvian Government led by President Juan Velasco Alvarado and the efforts of Panama to consolidate its territorial integrity. The NAM leaders agreed "that the realisation of Latin America's full and true independence is an essential element in the general emancipation process of the developing countries and in the strengthening of international peace and security".[31]

Three new members from Latin America — Argentina, Chile and Peru – joined the movement during the Algiers Summit (1973). As far as Latin American issues are concerned, they figured prominently in the Algiers Declaration. However, Cuban leader Fidel Castro forcefully countered the theory of the two imperialisms. The radical and anti-imperialist tone of the Non-Aligned Movement was quite visible. The conference called for an end to colonial domination in Latin America, supported Puerto Ricans' demand for independence, and the dismantling of military bases in Cuba, Panama and Puerto Rico. The conference expressed solidarity with the Chilean Government led by Salvador Allende, hailed the victory of the Argentine people in the struggle for an authentic independence and social progress, and supported Panama's claim to sovereignty over the Canal zone. The radicalisation of NAM and Fidel Castro's clear imprint on Latin American themes were evident from a paragraph which said: "the struggle for the liberation of Latin America is an important factor in the struggle of peoples against colonialism, neo-colonialism and imperialism…"[32] Castro's denunciation of the theory of two imperialisms came to embody the general political problem of the orientation of NAM in subsequent years.

Meeting for the first time in Havana in March 1975, the Co-ordinating Bureau of the Non-Aligned countries recognised "the arduous efforts made by the people of Cuba to achieve full independence and economic development" and saluted "the victories won by the Cuban people in this exacting struggle". Interestingly, while the Latin American countries had broken off with Cuba and had serious reservations about the Castroist influence over NAM, the Co-ordinating Bureau was "pleased to have had the opportunity of meeting in Latin America" which, it said, had "written glorious pages in the history of struggle against colonialism, neo-colonialism and imperialism".[33]

Like Fidel Castro of Cuba, who moulded the deliberations of the NAM Co-ordinating Bureau meeting in Havana in his favour, the "revolutionary" Government of Peru under Juan Velasco Alvardo, who came to power in 1968 through a military coup, managed to have several paragraphs devoted to Peru, eulogising the military regime. The sober and pragmatic tone of earlier meetings was gradually replaced by stridently defiant postures towards the West. For example, the Lima Declaration said: "Latin America is one of the areas which has suffered the most from the aggression of colonialism and imperialism". It further said, that "the campaign of aggression in Latin America" is being carried on "by the agents of imperialism and by transnational enterprises".

The Lima Declaration complimented Peru as a Non-Aligned country which actively participates in the movement and "contributes to the cause of the liberation of Latin America and of the Third World, and to the *strengthening of the policy of non-alignment through a revolutionary process....*"[34] Again, while there were only four full members of NAM who attended the Lima Conference, the meeting viewed "with satisfaction the growing participation of Latin America in the Non-Aligned Movement". The countries in Latin America, it further said, "have an ever growing awareness of belonging to the Third World and of their common identity with the people of Africa, Asia and other parts of the world."[35] Such claims were hollow – long on rhetoric and short on substance.

Some of the other issues which figured prominently in the Lima Declaration included NAM's support for Mexican President Luis Echeverria's Charter of Economic Rights and Duties of Nations, Latin American Economic System (SELA), the economic integration and co-operation process in the region. Argentina's claim over the Malvinas Islands and the so-called nationalist and independent measures by Ecuador, Venezuela, Colombia, Panama, Mexico and Honduras to recover their natural resources.

By the time the Colombo Summit (1976) was held, the number of the Non-aligned countries had increased from 25 to 86. However, only seven countries were from Latin America and the Caribbean. Panama was the only new member from the region. Chile, suspended in 1973 following the military coup, was not invited to attend the Summit. The Colombo Declaration reiterated the stand of the earlier summit, using almost the same language to express solidarity with Cuba, Panama,

Puerto Rica, Guyana, Jamaica and Barbados, and paid homage to Salvador Allende.

The 1979 NAM Summit in Havana marked the culmination of the process of Latin Americanisation of the Movement. Four new members from Latin America - Bolivia, Nicaragua, Surinam and Grenada attended the Havana Summit. By now NAM had become a global force to reckon with and it had 95 members. Eleven countries from Latin America and the Caribbean (Argentina, Bolivia, Cuba, Grenada, Guyana, Jamaica, Nicaragua, Panama, Peru, Surinam and Trinidad & Tobago) were now full members, eleven more attended the summit as observers (Barbados, Brazil, Colombia, Costa Rica, Dominica, Ecuador, El Salvador, Mexico, St Lucia, Uruguay and Venezuela) and two with special status (Belize and Puerto Rico). Guatemala, Honduras, Paraguay and Chile were the only four countries which remained outside the Movement.

As Luis Maira maintains, "the sixth Summit can be said, without qualification, to have marked the integration of Latin America into the Non-Aligned fraternity, to a point where intractable governments will find it a decidedly negative factor to stay out".[36] For the first time Latin America occupied the centrestage in the Movement. Of the six new members admitted into NAM, three were Latin American (Nicaragua, Bolivia and Surinam). And of four new comers approved as observers, three were from Latin America and the Caribbean – Dominica, Costa Rica and St. Lucia. Latin American countries, formerly with four seats on the Co-ordinating Bureau, now had five seats.

Whereas in initial years Cuba needed the Non-aligned Movement "in its search for international political support, its successful internal stabilisation made it a very self-confident member of this group".[37] However, Cuba's simultaneous membership in the community of Latin America nations, in the Socialist camp, and in the Non-Aligned Movement were factors which prompted the United States to exert pressures simultaneously on friendly governments in Latin America, on the Soviet Union, and on Non-Aligned countries. Cuba's decision to send the expeditionary troops to Angola in 1975 and the Horn of Africa in 1978 further polarised the NAM countries. In the 1978 Ministerial conference at Belgrade, Ghana, Morocco, Somalia and Senegal accused Cuba of acting as Soviet tool. Egypt and Somalia even demanded the cancellation of the NAM Summit in Havana.[38]

Cuba's ideological activism at the Havana Summit brought to the surface serious internal divisions within the movement on regional and ideological matters which eventually weakened the movement. Three groups emerged with distinct positions. The one group reflecting the interests of the Western powers led by Zaire, Senegal, Singapore and Saudi Arabia vehemently opposed Cuba's efforts to take NAM closer to the Soviet Union. The Singapore representative indirectly accused Havana of toeing Moscow's line. He said: "Some of us have…picked up the bad habits of our former masters. We dream of empires of our own and solicit the aid of great powers to realise these dreams".[39] The second group led by socialist countries like Vietnam, Ethiopia, Mozambique, Cuba and Nicaragua emphasised the movement's anti-imperialist and anti-colonial character but actually promoted the concept that socialist countries be considered "natural allies" of the Non-Aligned Movement. However, the third group led by India, Yugoslavia, Sri Lanka and Zambia stood for strict adherence to the movement's original principles as defined at Belgrade.

Three more Latin American countries – Bahamas, Colombia and Ecuador became full members of NAM during the New Delhi Summit (1983). Venezuela joined the group in 1989. Brazil, Mexico and Uruguay have opted to remain as observers and have no intention to join NAM. In fact Brazil has been an observer since 1961 and Mexico and Uruguay since 1964. In 1995 Colombia hosted the NAM Summit. But its lacklustre leadership and a rethinking about NAM's relevance in the post-Cold War era have forced the movement to search for a new rationale to survive.

V. Mexican, Argentine Models

If one accepts Krishna Menon's definition that "a Non-Aligned nation must be Non-Aligned with the Non-aligned to be truly Non-aligned", Mexico alone could qualify as a Non-Aligned country in the world. It has refused to join NAM even though its foreign policy has a typical stamp of Non-Alignment. Mexico has also refused to join the Organisation of Petroleum Exporting Countries (OPEC) as also to commit itself to the General Agreement on Trade and Tariffs (GATT). According to one analyst, "Mexico clearly desires to develop its own foreign policy independent of the restrictions of these controversial and politicised multilateral organisations".[40]

Mexico has developed a diplomatic tradition, which is unique in the world. Soon after independence in 1821, Mexico became a victim of US and European expansionism. It actually lost half its territory to the US. Mexico therefore propounded a pacifist foreign policy doctrine which can be summed up using Benito Juarez's apothegm, "among individuals as also among the nations, peace is respect for other people's rights".[41] The Mexican Revolution of 1910 also gave impetus to a doctrine which kept the country outside the imperialist orbit.

The Lazaro Cardenas regime made an opening to the world by condemning the fascist regimes in Europe and opened its doors to Spanish refugees during the civil war. But Mexico dissociated itself from the alliance systems and strategic level defence initiatives. It even refused to sit on the Security Council during the Cold War. Mexico of course did not formally join the Non-Aligned Movement in Belgrade in 1961. But President Lopez Mateos (1958-64) did establish cordial ties with the Third World. He visited India, Yugoslavia and Indonesia to establish a personal rapport with Nehru, Tito and Sukarno, founding leaders of NAM.

Mexico has also continually opposed the concept of a multilateral hemispheric defence organisation and has steadfastly refused to participate in or condone any collective occupation force in the region as some Latin American nations did during the 1965 OAS intervention in the Dominican Republic. Mexico supported the Leftist Arbenz regime in Guatemala and opposed the 1954 US intervention to remove that government from power. Mexico's refusal to sever diplomatic ties with Cuba after Castro's proclamation of Cuba as a Marxist-Leninist regime in the early 1960s is the best example of the country's independent foreign policy. Mexico is the only country which refused to abide by the OAS decision in this respect.

Sometimes Mexico has pursued a quasi-isolationist policy in foreign relations. On other occasions, it has followed a radical and defiant foreign policy stances. As we have noted earlier, Mexico's nationalistic, anti-imperialistic pronouncements have been often aimed at neutralising its domestic compulsions. Luis Echeverria's Third Worldist policy well illustrates the point.

After its integration with NAFTA, Mexico appears keener to foster a "mature relationship" with the US, "characterised by an unprecedented level of co-operation". Mexico today is interested more in its integration with the multilateral and regional agencies like the WTO, OECD and APEC than NAM and the G-15, etc. And yet, even during the crisis period, between September 1995 and August 1996, Mexico worked on more than 1300 bilateral and regional assistance projects with Central American and Caribbean countries. Other countries that benefited from Mexico's assistance include Bolivia, Paraguay and Peru.[42]

Latin American States have been described as the 'Achilles heel' of the Third World movement. These States have often shown an inclination to break ranks with the Third World when their desired national interests come in conflict with the larger Third World solidarity imperatives. Nowhere is it truer than in the case of Argentina. Milenky characterises Argentina's tendency to implement both pro-Western and pro-Third World policy as "opportunistic" As he says, "Argentina wants to challenge the international political and economic status quo and to benefit from it. It seeks trade and investment from the industrial powers and then joins the underdeveloped nations to force changes in the rules. It seeks to be alternatively or simultaneously Western and Third World".[43]

Argentina's conflicting perspectives in foreign policy are not hard to explain. Till 1930, the Argentine political system was characterised by a degree of political stability, almost unknown in Latin America and by a level of economic development with a standard of living comparable to that of southern Europe.[44] Argentina's goal since then has been the acquisition of First World status. In the 1940s, Juan Domingo Peron expounded a foreign policy doctrine which came to be known as *la tercera posicion*, steering clear of alignments with superpowers. Though Argentina was the last of the Latin American countries to ratify the 1947 Inter-American Treaty of Reciprocal Assistance, also known as the Rio Pact, it has remained a trusted ally of the US all these years.

Following the 1962 Missile Crisis a combined quarantine force was established under a US commander in line with the objectives of the Rio Pact. It included two Argentine destroyers. Again in 1965 when the OAS authorised the establishment of a temporary Inter-American PeaceKeeping Force, Argentina was keen to join the force but domestic opposition prevented it from doing the same. In the 1960s, Argentina joined the US in joint military exercises, known as "Operation UNITAS".[45] In the late 1970s and early 1980s, Argentina came under severe criticism from diverse sectors for acting as US ally in Central America. It not only supported the Honduran regime but also provided training to contra forces pitted against the Sandinista regime in Nicaragua.

This is not to suggest that there were no differences between Buenos Aires and Washington. However, that was primarily to assert its own aspirations for regional pre-eminence. In the wake of the Soviet invasion of Afghanistan, Argentina refused to join the US grain embargo against Moscow. Here again, the objective of the military regime was not to provoke the US but to spare the government from castigation by the communist countries and others for human rights violations.

The Malvinas crisis of 1982 radically transformed Argentine foreign policy. Argentina was earlier contemplating to withdraw from the Non-Aligned Movement. Nicanor Costa Mendez wrote in 1979 that Argentina had very little to do with NAM and it "must affirm its faith in the West".[46] During the Malvinas crisis Argentina again discovered that it was indeed a Third World country. The same Costa Mendez, who was the Foreign Minister during the military conflict with Britain, rushed to Cuba to embrace Fidel Castro, who was the chairman of NAM. A country which was about to withdraw from NAM and had never been represented by its President at NAM Summits changed tack. It was thanks to the so-called "Malvinisation" of the Argentine foreign policy that president Gen Reinaldo Bignone personally attended the NAM summits in New Delhi and Belgrade in subsequent years.

Argentina under President Carlos Menem has withdrawn from NAM, and has become one of the United States' closest allies. Menem has not only turned Peronism on its head, he has all but thrown himself on the US doorstep. Over the years, an eager-to-please Menem has offered more than the US has demanded. The US, for instance, did not request Argentine troops in the Persian Gulf, but Menem sent them anyway. Argentina also sent peace-keeping forces to Haiti, Croatia and half a dozen other conflict zones. At Washington's urging Argentina has shut down its Condor II missile project and formed a special anti-narcotics unit along the lines of the US Drug Enforcement Administration. The closer ties with the US, dubbed "carnal relations by Argentine Foreign Minister Guido Di Tella, have also been characterised by clear support of the US policy towards Cuba. The Menem regime has broken ranks with Latin American allies to vote for a UN resolution to investigate human rights violations in Cuba.

Argentina considers itself to be part of the Western fraternity. As Guido Di Tella said, "we have left the group of Non-Aligned countries and joined the camp of Western nations, which are fewer in number but more important".[47] According to Menem, Argentine policy 'is guided by realistic and pragmatic principles; our only aspiration is to play our proper international role without ideological commitments which have no meaning in the world today".[48] Menem further said, "I don't stop to think in terms of Left and Right or 'comic opera nationalism,' – as Peron used to say". He has defended his alliance with the US by saying "adding poverty to poverty makes no sense; adding up the millions of dollars in foreign debt among Latin American countries with no capital in sight to help us out of this situation doesn't make sense either....We have the resources, and it (US) has the capital".[49]

The US has given Argentina a "major non-NATO ally" status. The first Latin American country to receive the distinction, Argentina will now be placed on a similar footing as Israel, Egypt and Japan. It will give Argentina access to surplus NATO hardware and US weapons.

Mexico and Argentina may provide contrasting models of foreign policy behaviour, but in the post-Cold War era, the objective of both the countries as also others is the same: attaining the First World status, Mexico through its membership of NAFTA and Argentina through its total identification with the West. The experiences of the past few years would seem to suggest that they may well be chasing a chimera.

Notes and References

1. M S Rajan, *The Future of Non-Alignment and the Non-Aligned Movement: Some Reflective Essays* (New Delhi: Konark Publishers, 1990), p. 3.

2. Junius Richard Jayewardene in his report as outgoing Chairman of NAM, *Sixth Conference of Heads of State or Government of Non-Aligned Countries, Addresses,* (Havana: Editorial de Ciencias Sociales, 1980), p. 55.

3. *Ibid,* p. 292.

4. *Ibid,* p. 27.

5. *Ibid,* p. 136.

6. *Ibid,* p. 197.

7. Simon Pierre Kibanda, Permanent Representative of the Central African Empire to the UN, *Ibid,* p. 158.

8. *Ibid,* p. 244.

9. Samora Machel, "We must Create our own Future", *Third World* (Mexico City), No. 3, November 1979, p. 36.

10. *Ibid,* p. 37.

11. Julius Nyerere, "A Definition of Non-alignment" *Ibid,* p. 42.

12. Joutros Boutros-Ghali, *Sixth Conference of Heads of State or Government of Non-aligned Countries, Op. Cit.,* p. 188.

13. Sinnathamby Rajaratnam in *Ibid,* p. 642 .

14. K Natwar Singh, "Essence of Non-Alignment" *The Hindustan Times,* April 7, 1997.

15. *Ibid.*

16. Uldaricio Figueroa Pla, *Organismos Internacionales* (Santiago: Editorial Juridica de Chile, 1991), p. 875.

17. Roeslan Abdulgani, cited in Sunanda K.Datta-Ray, "What is in a NAM", *The Telegraph* (Calcutta), 29 April, 1995.

18. M S Rajan, *Op. Cit.*, pp. 1-2.

19. *Ibid*, p. 2.

20. See President Tito's welcome speech, *Documents of the Gatherings of Non-Aligned Countries, 1961-1973* (Belgrade, 1973), p. 5.

21. *Ibid.*

22. *Ibid*, p. 6.

23. For a detailed analysis of Peronism, see Juan Domingo Peron, *La Hora de los Pueblos* (Buenos Aires: Norte, 1968); Eva Peron, *Historia del Peronismo* (Buenos Aires: Ediciones Mundo Peronista, 1995) and Roberto Aizcorbe, *Argentina: The Peronist Myth* (Hicksville, N Y: Exposition Press, 1975).

24. See Cavandoli's Speech at the Havana Summit, *Sixth Conference of Heads of State or Government of Non-Aligned Countries, Op. Cit.*, p. 90.

25. Uldaricio Figueroa Pla, *Organismos Internacionales, Op. Cit.*, p. 879.

26. The Belgrade Declaration, *Documents of the Gatherings of Non-Aligned Countries, 1961-1973, Op. Cit.*, p. 17.

27. *Ibid*, pp. 15-16.

28. The programme for Peace and International Co-operation, *Documents of the Gatherings of Non-aligned Countries, 1961-1973, Op. Cit.*, pp. 43,45, 47.

29. Tatiana Goncharova, "Aspectos Politicos e Ideologicos del Movimiento de Paises No-Alineados", *America Latina* (Moscow), No. 10, October 1982, p. 44.

30. Demetrio Boersner, *Relaciones Internacionales de America Latina* (Caracas: Editorial Nueva Sociedad, 1990), p. 15.

31. The Georgetown Declaration, Documents of the *Gatherings of Non-Aligned Countries, 1961-1979*, (New Delhi, 1981), p. 73.

32. Political Declaration adopted in Algiers, *Ibid*, p. 93.

33. Lima Programme on Mutual Assistance on Solidarity in *Ibid*, p. 144.

34. *Ibid*, Emphasis added by the author.

35. *Ibid.*

36. Luis Maira, "Latin America: Strong Presence at the Summit", *Third World*, No. 3, November 1979, p. 21; Also See, "America Latina: Su Importancia en los Paises No- Alineados", *Estudios Centroamericanos* (San Jose), Vol. 34, No. 327, October-November 1979, pp. 990-994.

37. Wolfgang Grabendorff, "Cuba's Involvement in Africa: An Interpretation of Objectives, Reactions and Limitations", in Elizabetth G.Ferris and Jennie K Lincoln (eds.), *Latin American Foreign Policies: Global and Regional Dimensions* (Boulder, Colo; Westview Press, 1991), p. 143.

38. H.Michael Erisman, "Cuba en la Cumbre de los No-Alineados", *Politica* (Florida), Vol. 2, September 1979, p. 6.

39. Sinathamby Rajaratnam, *Sixth Conference of Heads of State or Government of Non-Aligned Countries, Op. Cit.,* p. 643.

40. John F Meshane, "Emerging Regional Power: Mexico's Role in the Caribbean Basin", in Elizabeth G Ferris and Jennie K Lincoln (eds.), *Op. Cit.,* p. 209.

41. Ivan Menendez, "Mexico y el No-Alineaminento: Caminos Paralelos y Convergents", *Boletin de Relaciones Internacionales,* Universidad Feminina, No. 1, May 1983, p. 1.

42. This data was provided by the Mexican Embassy in New Delhi.

43. Edward S Milenky, *Argentina's Foreign Policies* (Boulder, Colo: Westview Press, 1998), pp. 19-20.

44. Peter G Snow, "Argentina: Politics in a Conflict Society", in Howard J Wiarda and Harvey F Kline (eds.). *Latin American Politics and Development* (Massachusetts: University of Massachusetts, 1979), p. 105.

45. Jorge I Dominguez, "The United States and its Regional Security Interests: The Caribbean, Central and South America", *Daedalus,* Vol. 109, Fall 1980, p. 116.

46. *La Nacion* (Buenos Aires), 23 October 1989, p. 9.

47. Martine Jacot, "Menem Sees Argentina's Role as a Canada of the South", *Guardian Weekly* (Manchester), May 17, 1992.

48. Carlos Saul Menem, *The United States, Argentina and Carlos Menem* (San Isidro: Editorial Ceyne, 1990), p. 32.

49. *Ibid,* pp. 17-18.

5

The World Order Changeth: Agenda for the 21st Century

The post-Cold War world is on the cusp of a new political and economic paradigm. The defrosting of the Cold War has left behind a skewed world. The events of 1989-92 ushered in not just a new era in international politics but, perhaps for the first time in history a new international system, without a hegemonic war. Today the domination of the United States is so complete and so little challenged that the Americans have begun to turn their backs on the world. Marx and Lenin have been sentenced to the history books and political and ideological antagonists of yesteryears now sing from the same page. The entire world now accepts the iron-logic of market forces and the dictates of global capitalism including those States, which still swear by Marx and Lenin.

I. Paradigm Shifts

In the emerging new world order, cataclysmic general war among the major powers seems literally unthinkable. Yet wars among and within smaller nations are multiplying and becoming more intense and deadly. Wars of ideology and struggles for resources have been replaced by wars of identity. Wars of national liberation have been succeeded by wars of national debilitation. History is far from ended, and the world seems closer to anarchy than to order.

The post-Cold War world is facing paradigm shifts in many spheres. At the end of the millennium no one needs to be reminded of the breathtaking changes taking place in geopolitics, geoeconomics, technology, ideology, modes of production, lifestyles and culture. A fundamental restructuring of production, finance and communications that has taken place in the past one decade has tended to erode national boundaries and national sovereignty from outside. Two contradictory trends – the integration and fragmentation of States – seem to be following concurrently. In fact, deep tides of nationalist and sub-nationalist feelings and powerful global financial and market interests seem to be running in opposite directions.

At a different level, there are shifts and exchanges in identity "not merely beyond the nation-state, but beneath or below the nation-state". While there are "demands for a lesser role for the State", others plead for "greater State capacity, precisely in order to scale down the eventual role or volume of State authority".[1]

The post-Communist world has been a cartographer's delight. In 1989, there were nine States in Communist Europe. In the same physical space, there are now 27 States. Each one of these is attempting to use State policies to create a nation-state. But almost all the States are wrestling with the twin challenges. First, the economic crisis from which they are suffering. Secondly, all are facing a national crisis in which they are struggling to assert individuality within the shattered framework of a common economic space from which they all want to escape but which they are still doomed to share.

The disintegration of the Soviet Union and Yugoslavia have led many analysts to contend that several other nation-states, even democratic ones, will meet a similar fate sooner or later. Many of the nation-states of today owe their present shape to the collapse of the Ottoman, Hapsburg, French and British empires some of whom look set to break up again. So far the democratic nation-states have shown a resilience to survive. However, Canada, which has too much geography and too little history has only managed to avoid disintegration. Few countries round the world are indeed neatly filled by single nations. Some nations – the Basque, the Kurds, the Palestinians and Cree Indians have no country at all. On the other hand, there are millions of Hungarians outside Hungary, millions of Chinese outside China and a million Turks inside Bulgaria. The nation-state has also been debilitated and is rapidly losing power to various supra-national entities and even the transnational enterprises.

First it was the order that grew out of the Peace of Westphalia that lasted for 150 years, then came the 100-year-long system created by the Congress of Vienna and the Cold War lasted for 40 odd years. For several centuries world history has been written in terms of the struggle for influence among nations. However, it is not clear yet what aggregation of power will be the focal point of the next century: cultures, economic blocs, regions, subregions, tribes or revitalised nation-states. After a century of bitter struggle between the free market capitalism and centrally planned socialism, on the one hand, and between constitutional democracy and authoritarian rule, on the other, democratic governance today is ever more widely embraced as an ideal and market-oriented economic reforms are being undertaken in almost every country. However, democracy is in trouble in many places, even as its triumph is proclaimed.[2]

The Berlin Wall was a sullen symbol of the bipolar world of the Cold War. After its collapse, the world was left to re-order itself. That new order is only now taking shape. The triumphant celebrations that followed the collapse of Communism and the adoption of capitalism by most nations have long died down. There is a growing awareness of the tensions between global economic forces and those who seek to maintain a civil and human society; between global corporations and national democracy; and between efficiency and social contract. The economies of the First World countries like Japan is in a shambles. The so-called Tiger economies of East Asia are wobbling. All these have exposed the frailty of the emerging world order.

Political analysts are still struggling to define the new world order — or even to find a name for it. The term "new world order" was coined by George Bush who said prior to the Gulf War, "we seek new ways of working with other nations to deter aggression, to achieve stability, prosperity and peace".[3] He further said, the world "recognised one sole and pre-eminent power, the United States". And because it is "the freest nation on earth", the world "trusts us with power… They trust us to be fair, and restrained. They trust us to be on the side of decency. They trust us to do what is right".

The term "new world order" was quickly discarded, after Bush had used it as a slogan to rally support against Saddam Hussein. Bush's objective was to establish American supremacy in the post-Cold War world but he sought to couch it in lofty principles, very much the way John F Kennedy had done prior to the showdown in Cuba during the Missile Crisis. Kennedy said, "we are prepared to pay any price, bear any burden, meet any hardship, support any friend, oppose any foe, in order to secure the survival and success of liberty".[4]

In the period following the collapse of the Berlin Wall, the world saw many wars raging in Yugoslavia, and along Russia's southern periphery, as also elsewhere. The way all sides flouted international norms and defied the world body led French politician Pierre Lellouche to coin the term "new world disorder". George Bush's lofty rhetoric was turned against him and against the world of unrealistic euphoria that swept over the world in 1989-91. For the sole superpower the world became a more brutal and violent place. Idiosyncratic politics became the order of the day. During the Cold War years, the fear of nuclear confrontation was an important source of stability. Because neither superpower could defeat the other, their antagonism could not be resolved and a sense of cautious permanence was established. This led Lawrence Eagleburger to despair: "We are living in a world of random acts".[5]

II. Images of the New World Order

Academics, theorists and policymakers have, over the years, sought to analyse the emerging world order through a variety of models, paradigms, often contradictory. Robert E Harkavy after having exhaustively analysed the various models has offered seven discrete images of the post-Cold War world. These include: the three-bloc neo-mercantilist thesis, the multipolar balance of power model, the "clash of civilisations" thesis, the unipolar dominance model, the "zones of peace" versus "zones of turmoil" model, the "global village" model and the bipolar-redux model.[6] These models are, of course, not necessarily mutually exclusive. The following five models, based primarily on Harkavy's exhaustive analysis merit serious discussion.

(i) 'Yes, You are the Superpower'[7]

The United States has been brazen about winning the Cold War and it has been behaving as a victor. Even though there was "almost universal agreement that the root cause of the Cold War's abrupt end was the grave domestic failure of Soviet Communism" the "Reagan victory school" took credit for it.[8] According to Margaret Thatcher, Reagan's "decision to go ahead with the Strategic Defence Initiative (SDI)" was "one vital factor in the ending of the Cold War".[9]

The present century may not have begun as an 'American Century' but it is certainly ending as one and its position is unlikely to be seriously challenged for a substantial number of years in the next century. It is Henry Luce who first used the term the "American Century" in 1941.[10] The debate about the "American Century" and the rise and decline of the US is continuing. As Paul Kennedy says, "the appearance of books entitled *The End of the American Century, Beyond American Hegemony,* and *America as an Ordinary Power...* (predictably provoked) "responses (in the form of books) such as *The Myth of America's Decline, America's Economic Resurgence, Bound to Lead, The Third Century and America's Resurgence in the Asian Era".*[11]

A combination of economic dynamism, global military strength, lead in cutting-edge technology and the appeal of its mass culture gives the

US a truly global reach. "Only the United States has the complete mixture of economic, military and diplomatic powers to qualify as the superpower".[12] According to another analyst, "as the century ends, the United States remains not only the sole superpower that can fly its B-52 bombers 19,000 miles from Guam to attack Iraq on a moment's notice"….(and) "through the likes of Hollywood, Microsoft, and CNN, it also dominates the metaworld of images, icons, and information".[13]

Whether one likes the US or loathes it, the reality is that since the Soviet flag came down over the Kremlin at midnight on December 25, 1991, it remains the predominant economic, military, cultural and technological force in the world. It spends as much on defence as the next six military powers of the world combined. According to Huntington, "in contrast to other countries, the United States ranks extraordinarily high in almost all the major sources of national power: population, size and education, natural resources, economic development, social cohesion, political stability, military strength, ideological appeal, diplomatic alliances, technological achievement. It is, consequently, able to sustain reverses in any one area while maintaining its overall influence stemming from other sources".[14]

According to Paul Kennedy, the American armed services are "equipped to fight "smart" wars, using everything from Stealth bombers and fighters to AEGIS cruisers and sophisticated night-fighting battlefield weapons. Through satellites, early-warning aircraft, and an extensive oceanic acoustical detection system, its forces usually have the means to spot what potential rivals are upto".[15]

The US is still very much marooned in the Cold War and the world community is getting used to its "arrogance of power". Reagan justified the American bombing of Libya as "self-defence against future attack". The Clinton administration justified a missile attack on Baghdad on grounds of "self-defence" against alleged Iraqi involvement in an attempt to assassinate George Bush months earlier. The United States spends $260 billion for the military each year. The sum is justified "as necessary to fight two wars simultaneously on opposite sides of the globe" and it "exceeds the defence spending of all other major military nations combined".[16]

Despite the disappearance of the Soviet Union, there has been hardly any major cuts in the number of American ground divisions, Air Force fighter wings or aircraft-carrier battle groups. Instead, the Clinton Administration has rushed to expand NATO to impose what one analyst calls "mindless hegemony", a predominance for its own sake.[17] There are still 100,000 American troops in the middle of a now united Germany, defending a "border" that no longer exists. As Jonathan Power says, at century's end, the world is America's oyster. The danger of such power is the danger of those who always fly too close to the sun".[18]

"The centre of world power, Charles Krauthammer contends, "is the unchallenged superpower, the United States, attended by its Western allies". It is "unashamedly laying down the rules of world order and being prepared to enforce them".[19] If the Cold War provided the US with the impetus for asserting its preponderance by co-opting Germany and Japan into the anti-Soviet coalition, Washington's pre-eminence in the post-Cold War era has been achieved by manipulating the international system in its favour. According to the Pentagon's Defence Planning Guidance for the Fiscal Years 1994-1999, the US must prevent other States "from challenging our leadership or seeking to overturn the established political and economic order" and it must deter "potential competitors from even aspiring to a larger regional or global role".[20]

There are several analysts who foresee a gradual decline of America's power. In fact, prior to the end of the Cold War itself, some commentators began to talk of the next century as a "Pacific Century". Henry Kissinger, for instance, contends that the United States would remain *primus inter pares* as "the greatest and most powerful nation, but a nation with peers".[21] In 1985, Lester Thurow wondered why the British Empire lasted 200 years and the American Empire slipped over 50. In 1979, *Business Week* featured a cover story on American decline which depicted the Statue of Liberty weeping. In 1990, Jacques Attali, a key adviser to Francois Mitterrand, published a book that portrayed an American decline so steep that the future could be determined by a European bloc and a Japanese-led Pacific bloc with America relegated to the role of "Japan's granary".[22]

America's continuing domination in the 21st century will depend on several factors, such as arresting the decline in its educational system, social fabric and decaying infrastructure. The growing drug and gun culture in the US may cast a long shadow over the American blueprint for the next century. However, it is the demographic change and the differential birth rates and performance levels between White and non-White ethnic groups which may pose greater problems. By 2050, the Caucasians will become a minority.[23] Such a change will "exacerbate ethnic tensions, as between African-Americans and Hispanic-Americans (over jobs), or Asian-Americans and African-Americans (over educational access), as well as stimulate the racial worries of poor Whites". Besides, it will affect the American economy.[24] All the same, even if the post-Cold War world turns multipolar, in traditional strategic terms, the US will still be protected from most of the effects of international conflict. All indications are that the United States seeks an active role as a global superpower while avoiding the dreaded spectre of the global cop, wasting American lives and resources. In other words, America is keen to have global engagement which benefits it but it does not want to squander its resources on global gendermerie. American engagement in Bosnia has amply demonstrated that its interventionalist posturing was aimed only at appearing virtuous. This is what one analyst has called the "conceit of innocence", the bad faith that employs selfish rhetoric for selfish purposes.[25]

(ii) Dance of the Dinosaurs

The post-Cold War world has witnessed the markets emerge as the ruling international authority, more potent than any military or political power. When arrayed against any nation, including the United States they can impose previously unthinkable changes. The worldwide elimination of barriers to trade and capital, and the rise of communications technology, have created the global financial marketplace. Average daily worldwide trading in financial instruments now exceed $ 1 trillion. This is largely carried out by huge financial institutions with short investment horizons. They are beyond the control of any government. As one investment banker says, "we have entered an age of unprecedented financial power and risk. The strength of worldwide markets, already immeasurable, will only grow. Markets will be the dominant, worldwide force of the early 21st century, dwarfing that of the United States or any consortium of nations. And as with nuclear weapons, we are now permanently in their shadow".[26]

The end of the Cold War and the global advent of market economy make a return to multipolarity almost inevitable. According to *The Economist*, "each period of history has produced its own patterns of relations….among the world's powers and that some in the past have been near monopolies in some corners of the world (the Roman Empire or the Chinese Middle Kingdom), but never on a global basis, while others such as the Cold War have been temporary duopolies".[27] The United States, Japan, China, Russia, and Europe will define the emerging pattern of the 21st century. Since geoeconomics has largely replaced geopolitics, it is not so much the military capability as the economic strength and clout of a nation or regional grouping which will define the new world order.

Francis Fukuyama of the "End of History" fame says that the ideological conflicts that dominated the world since the 1930s will now disappear. These conflicts will be superseded by milder economic rivalries.[28] In the post-Cold War era, the ideological glue among nations has come unstruck. Alignments will now be along perceived economic interests reflected in regional economic groupings. While no lasting power alliance can be predicted, competitive economic blocs are already emerging. *The Economist* does not expect either a Europe-China alliance to emerge to keep Russia under control, or a US-Chinese alliance directed at Europe or Russia. But a loose alliance among Europe, America, and Russia to contain China is probable. A second likely scenario is an alignment between China and the Islamic world which may push Russia and Europe closer together.[29]

The three major economic blocs have already emerged which will be in constant competition: (1) A German-centred European bloc; (2) A

US-led Western Hemisphere bloc, centred on the North American Free Trade Agreement (NAFTA); and (3) a Japan or China-led Pacific Rim region.[30] The European Union appears to be the strongest grouping so far in terms of the member States' stable economic base and the systematic evolution of integration mechanisms. Later the European Union could rope in Russia and possibly North Africa. The NAFTA, too, is already in operation and it will gradually encompass the entire Latin America. As far as the third grouping is concerned, it is not clear who will eventually lead the Pacific Rim region. Till the Asian meltdown, Japan was the obvious leader, with South Korea fast making up with the leader. China is apparently growing with phenomenal speed. Besides, it has all the attributes of a global power. But its ideological rigidity and the possible collapse of its development model may upset the Chinese applecart.

In the entire scheme of things, the Third World countries have very little say and except for some potential regional or economic power, these countries are likely to be relegated to the status of "neocolonial resource zones to be courted by the three major blocs".[31]

Till the 1997 Asian meltdown, the East Asian economies were threatening to overshadow the other two blocs. Asian scholars and leaders maintained that Western society was decadent and that Asian culture, with its strong emphasis on family values and social discipline, was more conducive to stability and economic growth. Such a thesis was demolished by the economic meltdown. Today the Japanese and East Asian economies are wobbling. But as Edward Mortimer says, the developments in Asia are "still too recent for any confident historical judgement. It may yet prove temporary. Certainly, it is too soon to write off China as a potential superpower of the next century".[32] Besides, sooner or later, the Japanese and East Asian crises will have a bearing on the American boom.

For now Europe appears well placed on the "world economic chessboard" and it is bound to be a dominant economic power in the 21st century. As Thurow points out, the 'House of Europe' contains 850 million people "that are both well-educated and start out not poor".[33]

Much will depend on how fast the process of integration takes place and how the Russian economy performs. According to Harkavy, "the spectre of a growing fault line between Islam and the secularised West may raise questions about whether the incipient Eurobloc could achieve the preferential access to Middle East Oil...[34]

The US-led NAFTA is another big economic bloc which will eventually integrate the entire Latin American region. By 2005, it is likely to emerge as the world's largest free-trade zone, extending from Alaska to Argentina. However, Latin America is right now only weakly tied to the US. Washington's enthusiasm for pursuing regional free trade arrangements will depend to a large extent on the performance of both the United States and Latin American economies in the coming period. A significant downturn in the US economy or a worsening of unemployment is likely to provoke additional protectionist pressures and to constrain new foreign policy initiatives. Similarly, sluggish growth in Latin America will tend to dampen US interest in closer economic ties. Many consider Latin America as not much of an asset in global competition.

(iii) Clash of Civilisations Thesis

The third image of the future foresees conflicts emerging in the world along civilisational lines as propounded by Huntington. The "Clash of Civilisations"[35] thesis highlights the extreme importance of culture as a critical factor in the international social relations in the times ahead. As Huntington says, "the fundamental source of conflict in this new world will not be primarily ideological or primarily economic. The great divisions among humankind and the dominating source of conflict will be cultural...the principal conflicts of global politics will occur between nations and groups of different civilisations. The clash of civilisations will dominate global politics. The fault lines between civilisations will be battlelines of the future".[36]

For one thing, Huntington's categorisations of eight major civilisations appears faulty. There is hardly anything like Latin American civilisation. Latin American culture is a transplanted culture and the countries are torn between their pre-Columbian past and Western colonial heritage. Similarly, there is hardly anything which can be called uniformly African. The Slavic-Orthodox civilisation is only part of the Western civilisation unless, of course, by Western, Huntington means Anglo-Saxon.

Huntington's argument is weak because it is built on the concept of culture which has about as much concrete definition as a snowflake in June. What is occurring today is not so much the clash of civilisations as the clash of capitalist models. According to some analysts, a bipolar capitalism is developing, pitting mercantalists against free traders, the Pacific against the Atlantic, and China vs the US and Europe. True, in the absence of communism as an enemy, the West—and specially the US—may see Islam, particularly Islamic fundamentalism, as a new adversary. But the Muslim world is not only dependent on the West, it is too deeply divided. Besides, the conflicts in the next century will continue to be between the nation-states. The nation-states are far from doomed. The global alignments would continue along perceived national interests among nation-states irrespective of the civilisations they represent. Besides, the war over Kosovo represents a final nail in the coffin of the clash of civilisations thesis.

(iv) End of Geography Model

The protagonists of the "global village" thesis do not visualise any fundamental conflict either between nations or between trading blocs. They believe the world will be more integrated and it will be guided by global interdependence. Today, the world "shares the same images from film and entertainment: the same news and information bounces down from satellites, instantly creating a common vocabulary".[37] According to Kiran Karnik, the communication revolution has effectively "abolished distance, and made terrain irrelevant.... we are no more than a second away from anyone anywhere on earth".[38]

Information technology is creating a "woven world" by promoting communication, integration and contact at a pace of change that far outruns the ability of any government to manage. Territorial sovereignty and control on the movement of goods and people, the two attributes of the nation-states, "are being undercut by the communication revolution".[39] Global currency, bond markets, Internet, CNN and MTV are the new empires of mind whose images swamp our consciousness. The entire world is adopting the technologies, values, lifestyle and aspirations of the West.

But is the world going to become a "global village"? The content and the package the Muzak of the new communications order is offering would lead to the monopoly of a single cultural form. The culinary homogenisation and transnationalisation of beverage consumption patterns sought to be achieved by international giants may have led to the Cocacolisation and McDonaldisation of the globe. But it has also manipulated the entire socio-political and ecological context in which people in the Third World work, eat, drink and reproduce. The new information technologies are not "technologies of freedom" but a weapon of destabilisation and "information colonisation". The new fault lines lie not between civilisations, but between those who are surfing in cyberspace and those who are not.

(v) One Planet, Two Worlds

As a result of the global financial and communication revolution, communities and nation-states appear to have less and less control of their own destinies. As Paul Kennedy maintains, the gap between rich and poor will only further widen as we enter the 21st century "leading not only to social unrest within developed countries but also to growing North-South tensions, mass migration and environmental damage from which even the 'winners' might not emerge unscathed".[40]

The ever-widening gap between the rich nations of the North and the poor of the South will create a new duality in the world. It will be the central theme of international politics because it will be the single greatest threat to peace and progress in the 21st century.

While history has caused the paralysis of the Third World societies, the developed world is moving in the opposite direction. We have two worlds on the same planet: one world is toiling to stave off hunger, while the other, encompassing the developed North, is chomping at the byte to cross over into cyberspace. Kapuscinski calls it "one world, but two civilisations".[41]

Despite 50 years of decolonisation and attempted development, the gap between the North and South, rich and poor will be greater at the beginning of the next century than at the beginning of the present century. As Kapuscinski says, "American development is so dynamic and creative that, by the beginning of the next century, it will be a completely different world on this same planet. Every day, America is producing more and more elements of a completely new civilisation which is further and further from the civilisation of the rest of the world".[42] Octavio Paz, too, echoes a similar sentiment when he says, "the US was born rushing into the future. It was and still is, the Republic of the Future, built on an evanescent substance—time. It is, in fact, the perfect expression of modernity".[43]

Max Singer and Aaron Wildavsky make the most eloquent presentation of the one planet, two worlds model. As they say, "the key to understanding the real world is to separate the world into two parts – one the zone of "peace, wealth and democracy" consisting of Western Europe, the US, Canada, Japan, and the Antipodes, and the other comprising the zone of "turmoil, war, and development" which include the former Soviet bloc States and most of Asia, Africa and Latin America.[44]

At the global level, the old saw is still correct. The ratio of average income of the richest country in the world to that of the poorest has risen from about 9 to 1 at the end of the 19th century to at least 60 to 1 today. "Ironically, inequality is growing at a time when the triumph of democracy and open markets was supposed to usher in a new age of freedom and opportunity. In fact both developments seem to be having the opposite effect".[45]

While the protagonists of globalisation have sought to perpetuate myths like the poor catching up with the rich and growing convergence of rich and poor, in reality the gap in per capita income between the industrial and developing worlds has tripled between 1960 and 1993, from $ 5,700 to $ 15,400. The share of the poorest fifth of the world's population in global income has dropped from 2.3 percent to 1.4 percent over the past one decade. The proportion taken by the richest fifth, on the other hand, has risen. As James Gustave Speth of the UNDP says, "we are living in a world that has become more polarised economically, both between countries and within them".[46] The 1996 Human Development Report reveals that in 1995, 538 billionaires possessed as much wealth as 45 per cent of the planet's population combined, some 2.3 billion people. By the beginning of the next century, there will be about 6 billion people on the planet – of those, 1 billion will be wealthy, 1 billion will be well provided for, 1 billion will be poor, and 3 billion will be desperately poor.

The uneducated, unemployed, unskilled, unfed and unsatisfied people— the so-called un-people — will not remain silent in the 21st century. There will be serious questioning of the lifestyle of the rich being imposed on the poor as a paradigm of progress. More than 600 million people in 40-odd countries suffer from malnutrition, and lack even basic health care and proper education. The reason? The money which should be spent on these services is being used to repay debt or, in some cases, merely the interest on the debt. Eleven million children die every year from easily treatable diseases because the rich world lacks the will to provide the meagre resources needed to overcome this "preventable tragedy".[47]

The five models of the emerging world order discussed above are certainly not exhaustive and some of them are not even mutually exclusive. Despite the nearly entire world espousing liberalism and market reforms, the world politics continues to be complex and no single image or model can adequately explain the shape of things to come in the next century. The world economic growth appears to have followed a cyclic order. The growth economies of yesteryears have become doomed economies of today.

As Mark Twain so wryly advises, "It is best to read the weather forecast before we pray for rain". Yet, when it comes to geopolitics or geoeconomics, the experts are not particularly to be trusted. They have turned out to be little more than "astrologers of power". Who knows whether the Cold War will return? NATO's air strikes against Yugoslavia and t! contempt the only super power of the world has shown towards the UN are indeed ominous. Perhaps a nationalist Russia will join an economically formidable China or some resurgent Third World countries like India to threaten the West, and Japan might shift sides.

Times change, and our perceptions with them. Those who were earlier seen as good guys suddenly look bad; yesterday's bad guys are today's friends. The distorting prism though which foreign policy is often viewed has, in an age of shifting ideologies, demanded much refocusing of belief not only among antagonists but about nations on the periphery. We do know the 21st century will bring drastic change in the world order, but we do not know the character it will acquire. Our tools for understanding are too crude. One source of insight is the study of complexity, and another is the chaos theory. In both, there is confirmation that dramatic developments often arise from trivial events.

Notes and References

1. Philippe Schmitter's comment in a seminar *"O Brasil e as Tendencias Economicas e Politicas Contemporaneas"* (Brasilia, 2-3 December 1994) p. 36.

2. Ash Narain Roy, "Is Democracy Infallible?", *The Hindustan Times,* August 12, 1996.

3. "The World Order Changeth", *The Economist* (London) June 22, 1991, p. 13.

4. *Ibid.*

5. Lawrence Eagleburger quoted in Lester Venter, *When Mandela Goes: The Coming of South Africa's Second Revolution* (Doubleday: Transworld Publishers, 1997), p. 25.

6. Robert E Harkavy, "Images of the Coming International System", *Orbis,* Fall 1997, p. 570.

7. "Yes, You are the Superpower", *The Economist* , February 24, 1990.

8. Daniel Deudney and G.John Ikenberry, "Who Won the Cold War?", *Foreign Policy,* No. 87, Summer 1992, pp. 123-138. For further reading on the subject, see, John Lewis Gaddis, *The United States and the End of the Cold War* (Oxford University Press, 1992).

9.   "What Did We End the Cold War For?", in Nathan Gardels, *The Changing Global Order: World Leaders Reflect* (Malden, Massachusetts: Blackwell Publishers 1997), p. 89.

10. Paul Kennedy, *Preparing for the Twenty-first Century* (Hammersmith, London: Fontana Press, 1994), pp. 290-91.

11. *Ibid*, p. 291.

12. "Yes, You are the Superpower", *Op. Cit.,* p. 11.

13. Nathan Gardels, "Preface", The Changing *Global Order, Op. Cit.*.

14. Samuel P.Huntington, "The US: Decline or Renewal?" *Foreign Affairs*, Winter 1988-89, p. 91.

15. Paul Kennedy, *Op. Cit.*.

16. Max Frankel, "America Marooned in a Post-Cold War Trance", *Khaleej Times,* November 20, 1997.

17. Mark Danner, quoted in *Ibid*.

18. Jonathan Power, "No End to America's Arrogance of Power", *Khaleej Times*, November 15, 1997.

19. Charles Krauthammer, quoted in Ted Galen Carpenter, "The New World Disorder", *Foreign Policy,* Fall 1991, p. 27.

20. Christopher Layne and Benjamin Schwartz, "American Hegemony: Without an Enemy", *Foreign Policy*, Fall 1993, pp. 9-10.

21. Henry Kissinger, quoted in Robert E.Harkavy, *Op. Cit.,* p. 577.

22. For an interesting analysis of America's position vis-à-vis Europe and Japan, see Lester Thurow, *Head to Head: The Coming Economic Battle among Japan, Europe and America* (New York: Morrow, 1992).

23. W A Henry, "Beyond the Melting Pot', *Time*, April 9, 1990, pp. 28-35. According to some projections, by the year 2030, Mexicans and Latinos will dominate the population of the North American free trade zone.

24. Paul Kennedy, *Op. Cit.,* p. 313.

25. See Stjepan G Mestrovic, (ed.), *The Conceit of Innocence: Losing the Conscience of the West* (Texas : A & M University, 1998).

26. Roger C Altman, "Stronger than any Military or Political Power: The Global Financial Market", *Khaleej Times,* March 3, 1998.

27. "The New World Order: Back to the Future", *The Economist,* January 8, 1994, pp. 21-23.

28. Francis Fukuyama, *The End of History and the Last Man* (New York: The Free Press, 1992).

29. *The Economist,* quoted in Robert E.Harkavy, *Op. Cit.,* p. 577.

30. Proponents of the three-bloc neo-mercantilist thesis include Lester Thurow, *Op. Cit.*, Walter Russel Mead, "On the Road to Ruin", *Harper's*, March 1990, pp. 59-64; Edward Luttwak, *The Endangered American Dream* (New York: Simon and Schuster, 1993); and Jeffrey Garten, *A Cold Peace* (New York: Times Books, 1992).

31. Robert E Harkavy, *Op. Cit.*, p. 572.

32. Edward Mortimer, "Elusive World Order", *The Financial Times* (London), June 17, 1998.

33. Lester Thurow, *Op. Cit.*, p. 252.

34. Robert E Harkavy, *Op. Cit.*, p. 574.

35. Samuel Huntington, *The Clash of Civilisations and the Remaking of World Order* (New York: Simon and Schuster, 1996).

36. Samuel Huntington, "The Clash of Civilisations," *Foreign Affairs,* Summer 1993, p. 22.

37. Daniel Yergin and Joseph Stainislaw, "Sale of the Century", *Financial Times Weekend,* January 24-25, 1998.

38. Kiran Karnik, "The Emerging Communication Scenario", Vikram Sarabhai Foundation Lecture Series, August 12, 1996.

39. *Ibid.*

40. Paul Kennedy, *Op. Cit.,* p. 334.

41. Ryszard Kapuscinksi, "One World, Two Civilisations", in Nathan Gardels, *Op. Cit.,* pp. 3-8.

42. *Ibid*, p. 5.

43. Octavio Paz, "The Border of Time", New *Perspectives Quarterly,* Vol, 8. No 1, Winter 1991, p. 36.

44. Max Singer and Aaron Wildavsky, *The Real World Order* (Chatham, N.J: Chatham House Publishers, 1993), p. 3.

45. Nancy Birdsall, "Life is Unfair: Inequality in the world", *Foreign Policy*, Summer 1998, p. 77.

46. James Gustave Speth, "Global Inequality: 358 Billionaires Versus 2.3 Billion People", in Nathan Gardels, *Op. Cit.,* p. 166.

47. Hiroshi Nakajima, WHO Director-General, quoted in Noam Chomsky, *Powers and Prospects: Reflections on Human Nature and the Social Order* (Delhi: Madhyam Books, 1996), p. 106.

6

The Future of the Third World: Requiem or New Agenda?

Literature on the Third World in general and Latin America's role in Third World fora in particular is extensive and rich. However, not many scholars have incorporated empirical findings and theoretical reflections into an integrated whole. So while there is a body of knowledge about Latin America's peripheral role in the Non-Aligned Movement and other Third World fora, the field still lacks a firm paradigm. Since the disintegration of the Soviet Union and emergence of a unipolar world, it is no more fashionable to speak of Third World identity or Third World solidarity; these have gone out of popular lexicon. Suddenly the Third World has ceased to be a popular subject of post-graduate or doctoral dissertations. Is the Third World still there? Is it a concept whose time has passed? Does the Third World have a future? What role do Third World and NAM countries have in the new topography of power? What is the agenda for the 21st century?

Making an accurate prognosis about the shape of things to come in the 21st century is a complex and challenging task. The future is nearly impossible to divine. As eminent futurologist Alvin Toffler says, "anybody who claims to know the future is a quack". What he has done in his eminently readable books like *"Powershift"*, *"Future Shock"* and *"The Third Wave"* is only to find patterns in the chaos of the world.[1]

This chapter claims to make no effort to foresee the unforeseen. It only seeks to identify, understand and demonstrate the processes of change already underway in the Third World. There are inescapable elements of Third World's future direction contained in its present, and the book has only sought to unfold a vision of that future.

As the world is preparing to enter the 21st century a mood of cynicism, a pervasive feeling of powerlessness and a sense of being unable to connect with and engage in Third Worldism of yesteryears characterise the perceptions of a great many Third World countries. We live in anti-political times. That the Third World is in retreat and many States are busy redrawing their political maps are indeed quite apparent. The familiar maps of Third World politics are becoming anachronistic. Both its spatial and temporal boundaries are moving, blurring and even vanishing. The world is witnessing not merely political changes but a change in politics itself.

The way the Third World is drifting today resembles a journey without a compass. In fact, the plight of Third World countries can be compared to that of Christopher Columbus. They are off on a voyage across uncharted seas, bound for a land they don't know. NAM and G-77 summits take place periodically. Summit deliberations are still marked by self-congratulatory tone but they lack conviction. The maps the NAM countries are using today have become obsolete. Things are no longer what they used to be and the scales have changed. Time has perhaps come to revise the existing political cartography.

I. The Third World in Retreat

The Third World seems out of touch with today's world. Forums and movements like NAM, G-77 etc, are a relic of a very different era. Despite such a fate, writing an obituary of Third World would be premature. Even at the height of the Cold War, both the First World and the Second World were dismissive about the existence of the Third World. The Second World, despite the Third World countries being sympathetic towards it, did not recognise the Third World on the plea that there existed only two worlds, capitalist and socialist. Since the underdeveloped capitalist countries were tied insubordinately to the First World, they were indeed part of the First. But the First World did not do so either, maintaining that the Third World was no different from the Second.

Some analysts have proclaimed the end of the Third World. Others contend it has reached its end of history. Since the bipolar world is history and the post-Cold War world is facing paradigm shifts in many fields including ideology, economic development model etc, Third Worldism as an overarching ideology has reached a dead-end. No one believes in it anymore. According to John Toye, "the Third World exists only because it has been created".[2] He further maintains, "the creative force was not history or geography, or economics. It was psychology and politics of foreign aid, which between them conjured up 'the Third World.'"[3]

Such a view is too paternalistic and for that reason unacceptable. The market gurus maintain that the Third World is scripting its own failure . If the Third World countries believe their misfortune is someone else's fault, it is not entirely rhetorical. Third World poverty was, and continues to be, a direct consequence of the affluence, exploitation, and greed of the major industrial powers. As Patricia Adams and Lawrence Solomon maintain, the international financial, "have-money-must-lend" institutions are "one of the main causes of the sad state of economic affairs in parts of the Third World".[4]

To the Third World countries, the choice between tied aid and no aid was unenviable. The Western powers, particularly the United States used aid "as a Cold War tool…to promote political stability, win alliances and impede the emergence of radical or communist regimes".[5] In the entire post-war period, the Third World countries were of immediate interest to the US only because of Cold War considerations. America's fixation with many Third World radicals was primarily explained by their security ties to the Soviet Union. With the end of the Cold War, most of America's security concerns in the Third World have disappeared.

The debtor countries share part of the blame for their miseries. Corruption, mismanagement and war have wreaked havoc on many fragile economies of the Third World. But creditor countries, their banks and other financial institutions are not innocent either. There have been any number of cases of profligate lending, unreasonable repayment conditions, and the irresponsible transfer of arms. Whatever the history of today's debt-ridden countries, nearly all have one key fact in common. It is the poorest in these countries who have suffered the most and are the least to be blamed.

The terrible poverty at the global level is an ugly reality of the emerging world order. We have already seen how the plight of the poor and the marginalised people is getting worse. The real crunch is that the poor are getting poorer while the rich are getting richer. The rich-poor gap is widening, not closing. And it is happening all over, not just at the interface between the rich and the poor nations. The same dynamic is at work within countries, even developed and industrialised societies. In all developed countries there is a fringe of poverty. In the US, a new phenomenon has emerged since the 1970s—a semi-hereditary poverty which has created a new social class, the 'underclass'. On the other hand, Third World political and economic elites "are increasingly integrated into an international class structure". This led one analyst to argue that "in a sense we are all Third-or First-World now."[6]

The end of Cold War is not the only factor for the decline of Third Worldism. Third World ceased to be a single entity since the 1970s itself. As Hobsbawn says, "at the very moment when the Third World and the ideologies based on it were at their peak, the concept began to crumble."[7] What split it was primarily economic development and its consequences. The oil embargo of 1973 raised not only the prospects of Third World economic take-off but also a shift in the global balance of economic power. In retrospect, this was no more than an unkind chimera, comprehensively cast aside, outside of East Asia, by the new realism of debt and depression in the 1980s.

The structural adjustment programmes imposed on several African countries by the World Bank and IMF only worsened the social resources of these countries. The debt crisis crippled Latin American economies. Latin America's external debt grew from $ 354 billion to $ 470 billion between 1982 and 1993. The origin of Latin America's debt crisis goes back to the 1970s when US banks recycled vast amounts of oil dollars into foreign loans. It was assumed that rising oil prices would make repayment painless and that borrowers would use the debt for reforms by which to outgrow its burden.

The collapse in oil prices and a sharp rise in interest rates of the early 1980s shattered that illusion. Starting in 1982, first Mexico and then other debtors found it impossible to meet their obligations as some countries owed more than they could possibly repay. Between 1982 and 1988 Latin America paid around $233 billion in interest but its indebtedness only further increased by $850 billion. Latin America became a net exporter of capital.

The triumph of OPEC in 1973 produced a body of Third World States which emerged as fabulously rich not only in terms of per capita income but also infrastructure development and life-styles. Suddenly the poor, backward Sheikhdoms and Sultanates emerged as powers who had very little in common with the rest of the Third World. In the 1970s, OPEC shook financial markets worldwide. Its deliberations were closely monitored by the media and accorded a status normally reserved for superpower summits. Headlines like "the Cartel that has the world by the throat" (*US News and World Report*) and "Tomorrow belongs to OPEC" (*The Nation*) reflected a general perception of OPEC's growing international clout.[8] Today, the price in dollar per barrel of Arab light crude is a little lower than what it was before 1973. The oil price is now lower in money terms than it was in January 1974, immediately after the first oil shock.

The debt crisis in Latin America, OPEC's diminishing clout, a proliferation of wars of attrition between NAM members and the disintegration of the Soviet Union have all combined together to create dissensions within the Third World. As Hobsbawn says, "the astonishing 'great leap forward' of the (capitalist) world economy, and its growing globalisation not only divided and disrupted the concept of a Third World, it also brought virtually all its inhabitants consciously into the modern world."[9] The age of innocence is over.

II. Latin America and the Third World Drifting Apart

Latin America's tenuous links with the Third World movements like NAM have been adequately explained. The region's peculiar history, colonial legacy, its distinctive trade and investment patterns and, above all, the overbearing presence of the United States kept Latin America somewhat aloof from the rest of the Third World nations. Following the end of the Second World War and the arrival of the modern episode of decolonisation, any declaration of non-alignment by the Latin American States would have been construed by the US as a hostile act. Latin American countries perhaps knew perfectly well that the pragmatic course of action was to keep on the right side of Washington. The pilot fish behaviour of the Latin American countries was also guided by the oligarchic character of the regimes in power.

Latin American States have rightly been described as the 'Achilles' heel' of the Third World. They have often been found to be breaking ranks with the Third World nations depending on the exigencies of the situation. In the post-Cold War period, they are even more integrated with the US than they were in the initial years of the post-war period. While some countries are hoping to graduate from the Third World to the First World through regional integration and membership of NAFTA, Latin America is also forging an Iberian –American identity.

In Latin America, as in other regions, a sort of antipolitcs is gaining influence and even political power. The emergence of leaders like Carlos Menem of Argentina, Alberto Fujimori of Peru, Fernando Henrique Cardoso of Brazil and Hugo Chavez of Venezuela represent the new face of Latin American politics. Menem has not only withdrawn

Argentina from NAM, he has gone from denouncing *Yanqui invasores* (invaders) as early Peronists did, to luring *Yanqui inversores* (investors).

As Juan Corradi, a keen Argentina watcher says, Menem "a nimble showman plays the parts of playboy, sportsman and Caudillo, entrepreneur, unlike his predecessor he is uplifted rather than weighed down by his multiple role....He has transformed Argentine politics from stern moral drama to ribald vaudeville, full of scandal and pantomime."[10] Menem is perhaps Latin America's first post-modern President who exemplifies the new style politics of the region. The Fujimori phenomenon is another example of Latin America's flirtations with the politics of anti-politics. Fujimori is a micro-managerial President whose outstanding claim to a place in history books is that he had crushed his country's guerrilla movements. For a man who lacked power base, he attacked some of Peru's most powerful institutions. The judiciary, Parliament, military and the Church all felt his waspish tongue. If Fujimori called judges "jackals", he denounced the Roman Catholic Church for its "medieval and recalcitrant" stances on birth control. Under Fujimori neo-liberalism rules. On the other hand, with the victory of Hugo Chavez in Venezuela, the spectre of the populist demagogue haunts Latin America again. His vicotry marks the most significant move to the Left in Latin America over a decade. To Chavez, "social revolution is the salvation of the country." His promise to follow a more interventionist economic policy would mark a decisive break from the market-friendly policies of the past decade.

Latin America's behaviours vis-à-vis Third World perhaps represent more than simple deviant cases; they form part of a more general process of redefinition and restructuring of politics. More and more countries are abandoning the straitjackets of the past to embark on bold new initiatives, particularly economic, appropriate to present and future demands on the region.

It will be unfair to blame Latin American countries alone for casting off their Third World identity. For long, Third World was synonymous with poverty and economic underdevelopment. For the World Bank, the Third World comprises low income countries. The Third World solidarity was not meant to remain in perpetual poverty. Some Middle Eastern countries and, till recently, the majority of South East Asian economies have had a higher per capita income than do some of the industrial powers. Many of these countries were only notionally the Third World countries. India and Pakistan have now acquired nuclear capabilities. There will be many to question India's leadership of the Third World or NAM. India itself may be aspiring to use its nuclear empowerment to join the big power league.

In any event, Third World solidarity was never real. If the North-South dialogue failed, so did the much-hyped South-South co-operation. The oil rich countries failed to help create funds for helping the poor countries exactly the way the industrial powers did all these years. Whatever validity the poor nations' club may have had in the immediate aftermath of decolonisation, it has been weakened by changes within the Third World. Today, the economic position of Third World countries is more variegated than ever, with some having reached the point of being indistinguishable from developed economies, while others are retrogressing despite succession of schemes and strategies of development.

III. Structural Vulnerabilities

We live in a very different world today from the one experienced by early proponents of Third Worldism. The dynamics that make up the present day differ from those that applied in the 50s and 60s. The fundamental shifts in the world economy and the new ideological paradigm are driving the world in directions often unknown. Even a decade ago, much of the dialogue between the developing and the developed countries was ideologically coloured. Today, the terms of debate have been transformed by the emergence of trade and private capital flows as the primary engines of global economic growth, increasing pressure on governments to reform and liberalise. It is the neo-liberal "Washington consensus" which sets the terms for the rest of the world.

Globalisation, considered by some as "a destructive leviathan", has pushed many Third World countries on the verge of economic marginalisation. In Latin America, perceptions of the failure of neo-liberalism have prompted echoes in some quarters of pre-globalisation, pre-reform arguments that emerging markets in the Third World are either not ready, or else not suited for liberal economic internationalism. There may or may not be real backlash against neo-liberalism but the Third World countries can't afford to accept asymmetric globalisation. The way the industrial world has sought to impose and interpret globalisation, particularly the behaviour of free financial markets, implies a protectionism of the strongest in which perverse processes tend to turn markets into casinos.

All these problems require a more co-ordinated global response. International institutions such as the UN, the World Bank and the IMF are ill-equipped to provide it and in some cases, they have only further polarised the positions of the industrialised and developing economies. The Non-Aligned Movement and the G-77 cann't hope to fill the vacuum either. The fat has been stripped out of NAM and it is still not clear how it can create political muscle on top of its lean frame. Resolute political will and unity of action are keys to the eventual emergence of NAM as a force to reckon with, but these are commodities that remain in desperately short supply.

The international power structure is skewed and heavily biased in favour of the developed world. The industrial world and Western institutions dominate the international agencies and processes which have a bearing on the future trends in economy and international affairs. The Third World countries have little say in key decisions taken by global institutions. As Martin Khor rightly maintains, since votes are "weighted by equity share holding, the government structure of these organisations is skewed towards their major shareholders in the North."[11] The IMF, the World Bank and other Bretton Woods institutions, the experience of Third World countries including the so-called "Tiger" economies suggests, are the ones who lend you an umbrella as long as it is not raining.

The advent of the World Trade Organisation (WTO) has not improved things any better for the Third World. Despite their large presence in the

WTO, Third World nations continue to play a marginal role in the global body. The Third World countries represent a large majority of the world's population, but have less than one third of the total votes in such key international institutions as the World Bank and the IMF. Their advice is rarely sought by the developed world in crucial decisions relating to the future of the world economy. Unlike negotiations within the UN and UNCTAD, the Third World countries cannot negotiate collectively within the GATT/WTO framework. "The North-South negotiatory dimension", one analyst maintains, "does not exist and the alliances that are forged with GATT/WTO are built around a precise pole of interest rather than around a level of development."[12] While GATT covered export and import of goods and other related subjects, the WTO has a decisive say in services and intellectual property rights as well. Under the WTO framework the negotiating leverage of Third World countries has perhaps only further weakened. As Bhagirath Lal Das, formerly Permanent Representative of India to GATT, maintains, "the developing countries have been making concessions in the WTO without insisting on any reciprocal concessions. This has become so much the practice, that it is now accepted as a normal process..."[13]

The Third World countries suffer from other structural vulnerabilities. With the exception of a small number of countries, the economies of the Third World are dominated by agricultural and primary sectors with low levels of factor mobility. Vulnerability is therefore high. Falling commodity prices have come as a blow to the Third World. In the area of raw materials cartelisation efforts have failed. Once OPEC had the world economy at its feet. Today it is desperate to stop oil prices from crashing. Prices of other raw materials like copper, chrome, nickel, tin and tungsten too have fallen. Coffee exporting states have had sporadic successes in pushing up prices. On the other hand, manufactured goods of Third World countries face problems in export.

Third World exporters depend far more on Northern markets than industrialised countries do on manufactured goods from the South. The developed countries have import competing industries capable of producing the same products while the developing countries do not have alternative markets. To compound their woes, the developed world has used the instrumentality of WTO to undermine the comparative advantages of the developing countries in exports by introducing extraneous issues like the environment, labour laws, human rights and other social issues in trade and economic cooperation arrangements. Exports of agricultural products and textiles have been subjected to arbitrary proctectionist measures.

IV. Agenda for the 21st Century

The temper of the times in the Third and the First World in the 21st century will be realistic. The Government will be more concerned with economic growth than with ideology. Already a realisation has dawned on the Third World countries that there is no escape from the market-driven economy. But the poor countries of the world will be deluding themselves if they believe that by disowning their Third World identity, they will overcome their economic and structural vulnerabilities. Third World as a state of mind must be discarded. But the problems afflicting the Third World cannot be wished away by merely changing the label or embracing an ideology of untrammelled market economy.

The way globalisation has proceeded in the past one decade or so has only exacerbated differences not only among the Third World countries, but also within them. Heightened exposure to global markets has magnified and multiplied domestic inequalities. Only in a handful of countries, liberalisation and expanded access to global finance have resulted in significant advances in poverty reduction. In the bulk of the Third World countries, particularly African and Latin American, poverty has grown in both absolute and relative terms. In Latin America, wealth and income gaps, already the highest in the world in the 1970s, widened dramatically in the 1980s, a decade of no growth and high inflation, and have continued to increase even with the resumption of growth in the 1990s. In Latin America, the ratio of income of the top 20 per cent of earners to the bottom is about 16 to 1 and is almost 25 to 1 in Brazil.

High levels of poverty and extreme income inequality are not new to Latin America. Market economy would predict, though, that greater openness should have helped alleviate both: trade openness by promoting labour-intensive export growth and financial openness by expanding the pool of capital available for productive investment. But extremely fast-paced trade and financial liberalisation in Latin America have not helped reduce poverty or inequality. The globalising 1980s and 1990s have no doubt brought more Mercedes but also more homeless children to the streets, more Norwegian Salmon, but also more youngsters to the world of crime, more Nike sneakers but also more violence in and outside the home. Such a state of affairs will come under a renewed challenge in the 21st century.

In sheer statistical terms, Latin American economies are healthier now than any time since the start of the debt crisis in the early 1980s. Inflation, the main bugbear a decade ago, is under control. The continent continues to attract large quantities of direct foreign investment. Latin America's growth has averaged 4 per cent a year in the past decade, significantly faster than the average 2.7 per cent in the second half of the 1980s, but this has not translated into jobs. Real wages too have fallen. In recent months oil prices have fallen to their lowest point in 10 years, worsening the outlook for oil producers like Mexico, Venezuela, Ecuador and Colombia Similarly, the price of copper, which provides large chunks of export revenue for Chile and Peru, has fallen by more than a fifth since October 1997. After averaging 7.7 per cent annual growth for seven consecutive years, Chile, the so-called "tiger of South America" watched GDP nosedive in 1998-99 to an estimated 2 per cent as it suffered from the double effects of low commodity prices and high exposure to Asia.

If there is no improvement in the employment situation and if the income differentials continue to rise, the outcome could be a decisive political shift towards populism, nationalism and anti-Americanism. Latin American populism is the last refuge of traditional *caudillo* style leadership. To Latin American populists, faith in State enterprises and in the bogeymen of rapacious capitalists still retain its pristine virtue. It is at that point Latin America may again undergo a paradigm shift. Mario Vargas Llosa, one of Latin America's most popular writers, projects a similar scenario: "With the kind of privatisation now being generally pursued, the chief benefits of growth accrue exclusively to a very tiny elite. This is a big mistake because ten years from now there will be a reaction against the market and privatisation. Populism will then again find propitious ground in Latin America."[14]

Globalisation has so far provided only a Disneyesque beacon of light and a fake optimism to the poor. What Henry Wallace described the present century as the "century of the common man" which envisioned an egalitarian society remains a myth. It will remain a myth in the 21st century as well. The new topography of power that has emerged in the post Cold-War world is dominated by one peak. There are potential global powers and regional blocs trying to climb the peak. There are already signs of the growing differentials in economic growth rates producing dangerous fissures in many societies. When such divisions coincide with ethnic and religious differences, the result is likely to be increased ethnic antagonism and inter-group violence.

The phasing out of tariffs is hurting many countries. It is once again the poor, many of whom were overly dependent on artificially maintained commodity prices, who are feeling the pain. But their wails are being drowned in the din of the new world order. It may be a liberal order, but it is unforgiving towards those who do not, or cannot, play by its rules and meet its exacting standards. If efforts are not made to ensure that globalisation benefits extend to the 1 billion poor and 3 billion desperately poor people, there will be a crisis of confidence in the very structure of markets which they have embraced to overcome their misery. To some, the competition unleashed by global markets has resulted only in a race to the bottom.

The world's ability to confront these problems depends on increasing global co-operation and maintaining an international consensus in support of a just and equitable world order. This is where NAM and other Third World fora, however defunct or discredited, will have an important role to play.

The Cold War era was characterised by two types of global

divisions—the East-West and the North-South. While the East-West confrontation is over, the North-South divide has only further widened. Economic interdependence is the buzzword in the age of globalisation. In reality, Third World countries continue to be natural resource exporters whose products do not compete directly with the manufactured exports of the developed North. Interdependence of this sort "is a code word for continued dependence of the developing South."[15] Some analysts characterise the existing global economic system as "neo-imperialism", which is "at worst a Northern trick to cover up and perpetuate injustice, and at best a policy system producing unintended consequences."[16]

Today the industrial economies dominate the globe, as they have for the past 150 years or so. However, some Third World countries have achieved remarkable growth in the past two decades. Soon some of the industrial countries may be dwarfed by the newly emerging economic giants. History is testimony that such shifts in economic power are rarely smooth. Some analysts have already begun to see a Western conspiracy behind the recent Asian economic meltdown. Besides, the Western powers are taking advantage of the internal fights within the Third World countries. Samir Amin of the Third World Forum, Dakar, cites the example of Latin America: "There are no conflicts and yet countries are not coming together by forgetting their internal differences. The actual reasons are different economic interests of these nations which appear as the main hindrance for the alliance."[17]

What has largely happened with privatisation in most parts of Latin America is little more than the transfer of monopolies from the state to the largest private owners. This contradicts the moral reason for privatisation, which is the opening of markets and the creation of competition that will drive the process of wealth creation.

While the Third World nations were quite successful in uniting to achieve national freedom, they have utterly failed to unite for economic development. If war, famine and rain are the post-colonial legacy for too many Africans, Latin American countries are still wrestling with militarism, guerrilla violence, drug trafficking and growing economic disparities. One way to overcome the problems plaguing the Third World is to promote regional integration. If the developing world does not follow the path of regional cooperation, the lack of stability and growth will push it further into the desperate margins of global society.

Latin American countries have developed a fairly advanced framework of regional co-operation. The nine members of South America's two largest trade bloc, the Andean Pact and MERCOSUR, are all set to redouble their efforts to form a single free trade area. The four-nation MERCOSUR (Brazil, Argentina, Uruguay and Paraguay) and the five-nation Andean Pact (Venezuela, Colombia, Ecuador, Peru and Bolivia) form a market of 310 million consumers with a joint gross domestic product in excess of $1,200 billion. The five Central American countries and the Dominican Republic have signed a free trade treaty as a first step towards creating a regional bloc including the Caribbean islands. The bloc will comprise 22 countries when the members of the Caribbean Community are included.

Regionalism will be the key to the success of globalisation in the years to come. After all, regional agreements constitute the "building blocks" in the process of strengthening the multilateral trading system and of facilitating the globalisation of economic and technological relations. As Samir Amin says, "all The Third World countries need regionalisation which is a means to reinforce the capacity to negotiate globlisation".[18] Regionalism reflects collective solidarity in trade and gives to individual countries. Regional cooperation arrangements provide frameworks for what one analyst calls "lateral as opposed to vertical forms of development cooperation."[19] The regional integration process has so far been mistakenly restricted to trade. It must be broadbased to include political, social and regulatory issues. Globalisation is gathering plenty of enemies. Even its advocates accept that its benefits are not unalloyed. There are winners and there are losers. What the Third World countries need is globalisation from below and not globalisation from above.

The Third Worldism has to rebrand itself or die. In the new emerging world with relatively unknown rules of the game, the Third World countries need new and fresh strategies to create a political space for themselves. There is no point pursuing the line of Chinese fish, flipping and flopping to find its way back into a stream that has moved. Mad flipping and flopping by Third World countries will take them nowhere. The developing countries must hang together or else they will be hanged separately by the developed world. The experience with WTO isn't altogether happy. While the Third World countries are still recovering from the hangover of the Uruguay Round, they have been pushed to go in for a new round of trade talks, dubbed the millennium round, that would further open up their economies before results flow in from the Uruguay Round. The Northern countries have been circumventing rulings of panels and appellate body of WTO disputes. Their efforts to erect new non-trade barriers can be fought by the Third World only collectively.

Sadly, a sense of despondency and lack of enthusiasm in improving the ever diminishing bargaining leverage characterise the current trends in Third World. While some Third World countries have disowned their Third Worldism in the hope of getting better deals from the developed world, others accept their plight as inevitable and beyond redemption. As many as 87 of the 193 countries, mostly Third World, have fewer than 5 million people and little political and economic clout. They feel frustrated as individually they are too small to have an independent voice in world affairs. The Third World countries have the weight of numbers but they must stick together.

Third World countries share many things in common—diminishing economic growth, growing unemployment, high debt – servicing burden, balance of payments problems , falling share in world trade and adverse terms of trade and severe infrastructural bottlenecks. The significant dependence on foreign capital and assistance to fuel economic growth in the developing countries, especially the least developed countries, and the diminishing net inflow of funds from developed countries to most developing countries have intensified the need for greater South-South cooperation. Why has South-South cooperation not materialised the way the North-North cooperation has? The report commissioned by the Special Unit for Technical Cooperation among Developing Countries (SU/TCDC) puts it rather succinctly: "The contrast between what is available to the OECD (Organisation for Economic Cooperation and

Development) countries through their Paris-based secretariat and what currently exists for the benefit of developing countries in New York and Geneva is striking."[20]

The way globalisation has proceeded so far has left Third World countries as marginal players. The global crisis may strengthen the developing countries' desire to negotiate as a coherent bloc rather than as spokes around a hub. The time has come to explore new modalities of cooperation among the developing countries. South-South relations have to be built as a collective instrument to overcome Third World's growing marginalisation. To be effective participants, the developing countries need to understand fully the new opportunities globalisation brings and the new challenges it imposes on the development process. Globalisation has to be given the high priority on the agenda of the Group of 77 so that it could be managed judiciously. The new millennium summit being prepared by the Group of 77 is a welcome development. The idea for a South-South millennium summit was mooted in early 1997 at a G – 77 meeting in San Jose, Costa Rica, which was subsequently endorsed by its annual ministerial meeting. The central theme of this summit will be how to strengthen South-South cooperation and improve their development opportunity. According to the background paper prepared by the Geneva based South Centre, the millennium summit's key political purpose would be to assert and renew the collective presence of the developing countries on the world scene following a phase of ambivalence and inaction.

One way to strengthen their collective bargaining position is to place the G-77 agenda at centrestage in international trade and economic arenas. This calls for effective networking. The Third World countries have lost their trump card because they have not closed ranks. The developing countries cannot mark their presence, or have a say in global affairs on the strength of their sheer numbers. What they need is to devise new models of South-South cooperation. The logic and strategies of earlier times need to be modified. They should aim at solving specific problems of poverty, hunger, unemployment, sustainable development, recovery of natural resources and transfer of technology. To begin with, the Third World countries should take steps to forge cooperative links among a plethora of regional and subregional groups of developing countries. Ground realities, however, do not inspire much confidence. Rather than strengthening regional groupings and effecting direct cooperation among such bodies, more and more Third World countries are seeking membership of OECD, NAFTA and APEC.

More than ever before, the solidarity among Third World countries is needed. Roberto Savio, Secretary-General of the Society for International Development (SID), maintains that Technical Cooperation among Developing Countries and Economic Cooperation among Developing Countries (TCDC/ECDC) has an important role to play "in helping the countries of the South to work more closely together to increase national and collective self reliance."[21] The TCDC must address the plight of the least developed countries. At one stage the United Nations Conference on Trade and Development (UNCTAD) appeared an appropriate forum to improve and strengthen the Third World's terms of trade. It did negotiate a few commodity and producer-consumer agreements as also created a General Fund for commodities. But UNCTAD's efforts proved infructuous as over the years several developed countries withdrew from most of the agreements. Some have even suggested that UNCTAD should be closed down. Any attempt to reduce the role of UNCTAD should be resisted. The Third World countries need to strengthen UNCTAD as it can still function as an important think-tank for the developing countries. It can still play a counter-balancing role to the Bretton Woods institutions, and ensure plurality of thinking.

Demands have been made from time to time to make the World Bank more accountable and to return the IMF to its original function of short-term stabilisation rather than its current dubious role of policy enforcement. There are some who believe that rather than seeking a permanent place in the Security Council, the Third World countries must work for the creation of a UN Economic Security Council, a forum which could give leadership in economic, social and environmental fields. It would be more broadly based than the G-8 or the Bretton Woods institutions and more effective than the UN system. Third World countries could use the instrumentality of forums like NAM and G-77 to take the initiative in this regard.

It is equally imperative to strengthen the Third World's think tank capacity. In a globalised world key decisions affecting Third World countries are taken through international processes, conferences and complex multilateral negotiations where the developing world has very little voice. Unlike the developed world, the Third World lacks careful preparation, in-depth research, political commitment of their leaders and coordinating mechanisms. As Martin Khor says, "G-77 lacks a research facility or a permanent secretariat, and is unable to carry out long-term planning or strategizing for international meetings and negotiations." There is of course the South Centre in Geneva which has made major contributions especially during the UN General Assembly special session and the UN debate on reforms. But it needs more funds and stronger support from more Third World governments. The G-77 will do well to explore ways and means of strengthening its existing cooperation with the South Centre, Penang-based Third World Network and the Society for International Development (SID). SID, with its network of chapters and over 10,000 members worldwide, provides a useful forum for debate on issues of concern to the Third World.

In recent years demands have been made by various NGOs for the cancellation of the debt of the world's poorest countries, particularly sub-Saharan Africa. Salman Rushdie, India-born British writer, has proposed the cancellation of the Third World's debt burden as a millennial gesture of human friendship. In the context of their falling commodity prices and 35 per cent fall in grants and net official flows to sub-Saharan Africa over the past eight years, such a demand is valid. The Jubilee 2000, which is a coalition of churches, aid agencies and charities, is doing a valiant job in this regard. In the absence of a resolute political will on the part of individual Third World governments, the Jubilee 2000's voice will remain a cry in the wilderness. The G-8 countries in their Birmingham Summit in 1998 summarily rejected the debt relief arguments. Instead they agreed to a package of debt relief which in fact added very little to the existing arrangements.

However, there are hopeful straws in the wind. The Third World countries can bridge an enormous gap in power capabilities at the international level by intensifying efforts to transform the existing international regimes. Only by building or altering international institutions, rules, principles and norms, the developing countries can overcome their vulnerabilities and gain a voice in global affairs. The site of 50,000 strong crowd protesting at the G-8 countries' inaction over debt in Birmingham in May 1998 and widespread protests by farmers from India and other Third World countries in the middle of the financial centres of the world are perhaps signs of the coming times. It would be of course premature to read too much into such protests but the fact remains that in its own way the recent fracas at the WTO over the selection of a new chief is a sign that the developed countries can no longer have their way. Acrimonious recriminations, political smear campaigns and accusations of dirty tricks and double dealing at the WTO's Geneva headquarters are a symptom of a shift in the global political balance. If the developing countries succeeded in the exclusion of the social clause from the WTO agenda a few years ago, it was due to unprecedented unity in their ranks. Such a unity is the need of the hour today. The WTO's rules already cover areas as diverse as telecommunications, financial services and intellectual properly. A new trade round may add issues such as competition policy, air transport and direct investment. The G-8 nations' decision to whive an estimated $70 billion worth of debt held by the poorest countries and the so-called 'Cologne debt initiative' may have come as something too little, too late, but it would go a long way to help the Third World unite in their struggle for a just and equitable world order.

All said, the Third World countries have to strive hard to help foster international consensus on contentious global issues. Such consensus may prove elusive. But in a world short of suitable forums for seeking it, the informality and economic and geographic diversity of the Non-

Aligned and G-77 countries offer an opportunity which is worth seizing. As James Gustave Speth of UNDP says, "Let it not be said of our time that we, who had the power to do better, allowed the world to get worse. Human destiny, after all, is not a matter of chance, but of choice."[22]

Notes and References

1. Alvin Toffler, *Future Shock* (New York: Bantam Books, 1970) and *The Third Wave* (New York: Bantam Books, 1980).

2. John Toye, *Dilemmas of Development* (Oxford, Blackwell, 1993), p. 25.

3. *Ibid.*

4. Patricia Adams and Lawrence Solomon, *In the Name of Progress: The Underside of Foreign Aid* (London: Earthscan Publications Limited, 1991), p. 22.

5. Robert Packenham, *Liberal America and the Third World* (Princeton, N J: Princeton University Press, 1973), p. 5.

6. J F Bayart, "Finishing with the Idea of the Third World: The Concept of the Political Trajectory", in J Manor (ed) *Rethinking Third World Politics* (Harlow: Longman, 1991), pp. 51-71.

7. Eric Hobsbawn, *Age of Extremes: The Short Twentieth Century, 1914-1991* (New Delhi: Viking, 1995), p. 361.

8. Fadhil J Chalbi, "OPEC: An Obituary", *Foreign Policy*, winter 1997-98.

9. Eric Hobsbawn, *Op. Cit.*, p. 364.

10. Juan E Corradi, "The Argentina of Carlos Saul Menem", *Current History* (Philadelphia), Vol. 91, No. 562, February 1992, p. 83.

11. Martin Khor, "Globalisation and the Need for Coordinated Southern Policy Response", *Cooperation South* (New York), May 1995, p. 16.

12. Tran Van Thinh, "The North-South Dimension after the Uruguay Round", *World Affairs* (New Delhi), Vol. 1, No. 2, April-June 1997, p. 43.

13. Bhagirath Lal Das, "Repositioning Developing Countries in WTO", *Cooperation South*, No. 2, 1998, p. 58.

14. Mario Vargas Llosa, "Torture without Inflation", in Nathan Gardels, *The Changing Global Order: World Leaders Reflect* (Malden, Massachusetts 1997), p. 63.

15. Ismail Shariff, "The North-South Divide in an Emerging New World Economic Order", *World Affairs* (New Delhi), Vol. 1, No. 2, April-June 1997, p. 34.

16. *Ibid.*

17. *The Statesman* (New Delhi), February 4, 1998.

18. *Ibid.*

19. Stephen Browne, "Expanding Lateral Partnerships*"*, *Cooperation South,* No. 2, 1998, p. 82.

20. George Williams, "Expanding South-South Cooperation", Cited in David Delman, "Idealistic Notions for a Realistic World: The Case for South-South Cooperation", *Cooperation South*, October 1995, p. 19.

21. "The Future of South-South Cooperation", *Cooperation South*, October 1995, p. 6.

22. James Gustave Speth, "Global Inequality: 358 Billionaires Versus 2.3 Billion People", in Nathan Gardels, *The Changing Global Order, Op. Cit.,* p. 168.

Bibliography

Aguilar, Alonso, *Pan Americanism from Monroe to the Present: A View from the Other Side* (New York: Monthly Review Press, 1965).

Aizcorbe, Roberto, *Argentina: The Peronist Myth* (Hicksville, N.Y: Exposition Press, 1975).

Amin, Samir, *Capitalism in the Age of Globalisation* (London: Zed Books, 1997).

Anguiano, Eugenio, "Mexico y el Tercer Mundo: Racionalizacion de una Posicion", *Foro Internacional* (Mexico City), Vol. 18, No. 1, July-September 1977, pp. 177-205.

Attali, J."Lines on the Horizon: A New Order in the Making", *New Perspectives Quarterly,* Spring 1990.

Augero, Felipe, "Chile: South America's Success Story?", *Current History*, Vol. 92, No. 572, March 1993, pp. 130-135.

Benevolensky, V, *The Non-Aligned Movement: From Belgrade to Delhi* (Moscow: Progress Publishers, 1985).

Berger, M, "The End of the Third World", *Third World Quarterly,* Vol. 15, No. 2, 1994, pp. 257-75.

Bhalla, A S, *Uneven Development in the Third World: A Study of China and India* (New York: St Martin's Press, 1995).

Blasier, Cole, *The Hovering Giant: US Responses to Revolutionary Change in Latin America* (Pittsburgh: University of Pittsburgh Press, 1976).

Boersner, Demetrio, *Relaciones Internacionales de America Latina:* Breve *Historia* (Caracas: Editorial Nueva Sociedad, 1990).

Brandt Report, *North-South: A Programme for Survival. The Report of the Independent Commission on International Development Issues under the Chairmanhsip of Willy Brandt* (London: Pan Books, 1980).

Buchanan, Keith, "The Third World—Its Emergence and Contours", *New Left Review,* No. 18, 1963, pp. 5-23.

Calvert, Peter, *The International Politics of Latin America* (Manchester: Manchester University Press, 1994).

Cardoso, F.H. and Faletto, E. *Dependency and Development in Latin America* (Trans. by Marjory Mattingly Urquidi), Berkeley: University of California Press, 1979.

Castaneda, Jorge G, "Latin America and the End of the Cold War", *World Policy Journal*, Vol. 7, No. 3, 1990.

Chilcote, Ronald H and Edelstein, Joel C (eds.), *Latin America: The Struggle with Dependency and Beyond* (New York: John Wiley & Sons, 1974).

Chomsky, Noam, *Turning the Tide: US Intervention in Central America and the Struggle for Peace* (Boston; South End Press, 1985).

——————————, *Powers and Prospects: Reflections on Human Nature and the Social Order* (Delhi: Madhyam Books, 1996).

Continuidad y Cambio en la Politica Exterior de Mexico, 1977, Centro de Estudios Internacionales, El Colegio de Mexico, Mexico City, 1997.

Cruickshank, J "The Rise and Fall of the Third World: A Concept Whose Time has Passed", *World Press Review*, Vol.38, February 1991.

Cuadras, Hector, "El Tercer Mundo y Sus Lideres", *Presencia Nueva* (Mexico City), Vol. 1, No. 2, 1981, pp. 5-16.

Dani, Rodrik, *Has Globalisation Gone Too Far?* (Washington, DC: Institute for International Economies, 1997).

Das, Bhagirath Lal, *An Introduction to the WTO Agreements* (London: Zed Books, 1998).

——————————, *The WTO Agreements, Deficiencies, Imbalances and Required Changes* (London: Zed Books, 1998).

David, Steleven R, *Choosing Sides: Alignment and Realignment in the Third World* (Baltimore: Johns Hopkins University Press, 1991).

Davis, Ricardo Ffrench y Tironi, Ernesto (eds.) *Hacia un Nuevo Orden Economico Internacional* (Mexico City: Fondo de Cultura Economica, 1986).

De Soto, Hernando, *The Other Path: The Invisible Revolution in the Third World* (New York: Harper and Row, 1989).

Deudney, Daniel and Ikenberry, G John, "Who Won the Cold War?", *Foreign Policy*, No 87, Summer 1992, pp. 123-138.

Documents of the Gatherings of Non-Aligned Countries, 1961-1979, (New Delhi, 1981).

Dominguez, Jorge I, "The United States and its Regional Security Interests: The Caribbean, Central, and South America", *Daedalus*, No. 109, Fall 1980, pp. 115-133.

Duncan, W Raymond and Goodsell, James N, *The Quest for Change in Latin America* (New York; Oxford, 1970).

Duncan, W Raymond, *Latin American Politics: A Developmental Approach* (New York: Praeger, 1976).

Dynamics of the External Relations of Latin America and the Caribbean (Buenos Aires: Corregidor, 1998).

Economic and Social Progress in Latin America: 1989 Report, Inter-American Development Bank, Washington D.C. 1989.

Economic Commission for Latin America and the Caribbean (ECLAC), *Economic Survey of Latin America and the Caribbean* (Santiago, United Nations, Annual Reports from 1983 – 1997).

Erisman, H Michael and Martz, John D (eds.) *Colossus Challenged: The Struggle for Caribbean Influence* (Boulder, Colorado: Westview Press, 1982).

Evans, G Newnham, J, *The Dictionary of World Politics* (London: Harvester, 1990).

Ferris, Elizabeth G and Lincoln, Jennie K, (eds.) *Latin American Foreign Policies: Global and Regional Dimensions* (Boulder, Colorado: Westview Press, 1981).

Frank, A G, *Lumpenbourgeoisie: Lumpendevelopment, Dependence, Class and Politics in Latin America* (trans. from Spanish by Marion Davis Berdecio), New York: Monthly Review Press, 1972.

Fukuyama, F., *The End of History and the Last Man* (London: Hamish Hamilton, 1992).

Gardels, Nathan, *The Changing Global Order: World Leaders Reflect* (Malden, Massachusetts: Blackwell Publishers, 1997).

Gardner, Richard N, *Sterling-Dollar Diplomacy* (New York: Columbia University Press, 1980).

George, T J S, *The Enquire Dictionary: Ideas, Issues, Innovations* (New Delhi: Harper Collins, 1998).

Goldwert, Marvin, *Democracy, Militarism and Nationalism in Argentina* (Austin; University of Texas Press, 1972).

Hadjor, K., *Dictionary of Third World Terms* (London: Penguin, 1993).

Hakim, Peter, "The United States and Latin America: Good Neighborus Again?", *Current History,* Vol. 91, No. 562, February 1992, pp. 49-53.

——————————"NAFTA and After: A New Era for the United States and Latin America?", *Current History,* Vol. 93, No. 581, March 1994, pp. 97-102.

Harkavy, Robert E, "Images of the Coming International System", *Orbis,* Fall 1997, pp. 569-590.

Harris, N, *The End of the Third World* (London: Penguin, 1987).

Hayes, Margaret Daly, *Latin America and the US National Interest: A Basis for US Foreign Policy* (Boulder, Colorado: Westview Press 1984).

Hellman, Ronald G and Rosenbaum, H, John (eds.), *Latin America: The Search for a New International Role (* New York: Sage, 1975).

Hensman, C.R. *The Polemics of Revolt: From Gandhi to Guevara* (Allen Lane: Penguin, 1969).

Hey, Jeanne A K, "Three Building Blocks of a Theory of Latin American Foreign Policy", *Third World Quarterly,* Vol. 18, No. 4, April-June 1997, pp. 631-657.

Hobsbawn, Eric, *Age of Extremes: The Short Twentieth Century, 1914-1991* (New Delhi: Viking, 1995).

Hope, Sr, Kempe Ronald, *Development in the Third World* (New York; M E Sharpe Armonk, 1996).

Huntington, S. *The Third Wave: Democratisation in the Late Twentieth Century* (Norman: University of Oklahoma Press, 1991).

——————————— *Political Order in Changing Society* (New Haven, Conn: Yale University press, 1968).

Kennedy, Paul, *Preparing for the Twenty-first Century* (Hammersmith, London: Fontana Press, 1994).

———————————, *The Rise and Fall of the Great Powers; Economic Challenge and Military Conflict from 1500 to 2000* (New York: Fontana Press, 1987).

Kirkpatrick, Jane, "Us Security and Latin America", *Commentary,* Vol. 71, No. 1, January 1981, pp. 29-40.

Krieger, Joel, (ed.) *The Oxford Companion to Politics of the World* (New York: Oxford University Press, 1993).

Kurian, George Thomas, *Encyclopaedia of the Third World* (London: Mansell Publishing Limited, 1982).

Lowenthal, Abraham F, "Latin America: Ready for Partnership", *Foreign Affairs*, Vol. 72, No. 1, 1993, pp. 74-92.

Manor, J, (ed.), *Rethinking Third World Politics* (Harlow, Longman, 1991).

Manuel Perez Guerrero en la Escena Internacional (Caracas: Fundacion Biblioteca de Politica Exterior, Ministerio de Relaciones Extreriores, 1989).

Mayall, James and Payne, Authony (eds.), *The Fallacies of Hope: The Post-Colonial Record of the Commonwealth Third World* (Manchester: Manchester University Press, 1991).

Mecham, J Lloyd, *The United States and Inter-American Security, 1889-1960* (Austin: University of Texas Press, 1961).

Menem, Carlos Saul, *The United States, Argentina and Carlos Menem* (San Isidoro: Editorial Ceyne, 1990).

Meyer, Lorenzo *Mexico y Estados Unidos en el Conflicto Petrolero, 1917-1942* (Mexico City: El Colegio de Mexico, 1968).

Middlebrook, Kevin J, (ed.) *The United States and Latin America in the 1980s: Contending Perspectives in a Decade of Crisis* (Pittsburgh: University of Pittsburgh Press, 1986).

Miller, J D B, *The Politics of the Third World* (Oxford: Oxford University Press, 1965).

Molineu, Harold, *US Policy towards Latin America: From Regionalism to Globalism* (Boulder, Colo: Westview Press, 1990).

Morande, P, *Identidad Cultural de America Latina* (Santiago, 1990).

Munoz, Heraldo and Tulchin, Joseph S (eds.), *Latin American Nations in World Politics* (Boulder, Colo: Westview Press, 1996).

Needler, Martin (ed.), *Political Systems of Latin-America* (New York: Van Nostrand, 1970).

Ohmae, Kenichi, *The End of the Nation-State: The Rise of Regional Economies* (New York: Free Press, 1995).

——————————————, *The Borderless World: Power and Strategy in the Interlinked Economy* (New York: Fontana, 1990).

Packenham, Robert, *Liberal America and the Third World* (Princeton, N J: Princeton University Press, 1973).

Palmer, A, *The Penguin Dictionary of Twentieth Century History* (London: Penguin, 1979).

Paz, Octavio, *La Busqueda del Presente* (Mexico City, 1991).

——————————————, *The Labyrinth of Solitude: Life and Thought in Mexico* (New York; Grove, 1960).

Peng, Martin Khor Kok, *The Future of North-South Relations: Conflict or Co-opertion?* (Penang: Third World Network, 1992).

Pendle, G, *A History of Latin America* (Harmondsworth: Penguin, 1976).

Peron, Eva, *Historia del Peronismo* (Buenos Aires: Ediciones Mundo Peronista, 1955).

Peron, Juan Domingo, *La Hora de los Pueblos* (Buenos Aires: Norte, 1968).

Petras, James and Zeitlin, Maurice (eds.) *Latin America: Reform or Revolution* (Greenwich, Conn: Fawcett, 1968).

Philip, G "The New Economic Liberalism and Democracy in Latin America: Friends or Enemies?", *Third World Quarterly,* Vol. 14, No. 3, 1993, pp. 555-72.

Pla, Uldaricio Figueroa, *Organismos Internacionales* (Santiago; Editorial Juridica de Chile, 1991).

Popper, Karl R, *The Open Society and its Enemies* (London; Routledge and Kegan Paul, 1962).

Randall, V and Theobald, R, *Political Change and Underdevelopment: A Critical Introduction to Third World Politics* (London: Macmillan, 1985).

Robinson, William I, "Latin America and Global Capitalism", *Race & Class*, Vol. 40, Nos. 2-3, 1998-1999.

Roy, Ash Narain, "Fragile Democracies of Latin America", *Non-Aligned World*, No 14, April 1990, pp. 22-24.

——————————————, "The United States and Latin America", in Om Gupta et.al.(eds.) *G-15, Potential and Possibilities: An Indo-Latin American Perspective* (New Delhi: Pan Media,1993), pp. 81-89.

——————————————, "Global Expansion of Democracy" in M P Singh and Rekha Saxena (eds), *Ideologies and Institutions in Indian Politics* (New Delhi: Deep & Deep Publications, 1998), pp. 135-141.

Schutz and S Dorr, (eds.) *Global Transformation and the Third World* (Boulder, Colo, Lynne Rienner, 1993).

Segal, Gerald, *The World Affairs Companion* (London: Simon & Schuster, 1993)

SELA, *EL Impacto de la Crisis Asiatica sobre America Latina y el Caribe* (Caracas, March 1998).

Sixth Conference of Heads of State or Government of Non-Aligned Countries, Addresses, (Havana; Editorial de Ciencias Sociales, 1980).

Smit, T, "Requiem or New Agenda for Third World Studies?", *World Politics,* Vol. 37, 1985, pp. 532-61.

Smith, Wayne S, "Shackled to the Past: The United States and Cuba", *Current History,* Vol. 95, No. 598, February 1996, pp. 49-54.

Smith, William C, Acuna, Carlos H and Gamarra, Eduardo A (eds.) *Latin American Poltical Economy in the Age of Neoliberal Reform* (New Brunswick: Transaction Publishers, 1994).

St John, Ronald B, *The Foreign Policy of Peru* (Boulder, Colo; Lynne Rienner, 1990).

Stein, Stanley J and Stein, Barbara H, *The Colonial Heritage of Latin America* (New York: Oxford, 1970).

Third World: Development or Crisis?, Declaration and Conclusions of the Third World Conference, Penang, 9-14 November 1984 (Penang: Third World Network, 1992).

Thurow Lester C, *The Future of Capitalism* (New York: Penguin, 1996).

Toffler, Alvin, *The Third Wave: The Classic Study of Tomorrow* (New York: Bantam Books, 1981).

Torres-Rivas, Edelberto, *Proceso y Estructuras de una Sociedad Dependiente* (Santiago: Ediciones Prensa Latinoamericana, 1968).

Touraine, A, *America Latina: Politica y Sociedad* (Madrid, 1989).

Toye, John, *Dilemmas of Development* (Oxford: Blackwell, 1993).

UNCTAD, *World Investment Reports,* 1995, 1996, 1997.

UNDP, *Human Development Report 1996 (*Oxford: Oxford University Press, 1996).

Venter, Lester, *When Mandel Goes: The Coming of South Africa's Second Revolution* (Johannesburg; Doubleday 1997).

Willetts, P. *The Non-Aligned Movement: The Origins of the Third World Alliance* (London: Frances Pinter, 1978).

World Bank, *World Development Report,* 1995 (Oxford: Oxford University Press, 1995).

——————————————, *Global Finance, 1998* (Washington, DC).

Worsley, Peter, *The Third World* (London: Weindenfeld and Nicolson, 1967).

Yurlov, Felix N, "Shifting Patterns in the New World Order', *World Affairs,* Vol. 2. No. 1, January-March 1998, pp. 60-73.

Zapata, F. *Ideologia y Politica en America Latina* (Mexico, 1990).

Index

Author Index

Subject Index